WHY DOES MY DOG BARK?

How Mind Architecture Governs Behaviour

Fraser Beath McEwing

Published in Australia by Sid Harta Books & Print Pty Ltd,
ABN: 34632585293
23 Stirling Crescent, Glen Waverley, Victoria 3150 Australia
Telephone: +61 3 9560 9920, Facsimile: +61 3 9545 1742
E-mail: author@sidharta.com.au

First published in Australia 2021
This edition published 2021
Copyright © Fraser Beath McEwing 2021

Cover design, typesetting: WorkingType
(www.workingtype.com.au)

The right of Fraser Beath McEwing to be identified as the Author of the Work has been asserted in accordance with the Copyright, Designs and Patents Act 1988.

All rights reserved. No part of this publication may be reproduced, stored in a retrieval system, or transmitted, in any form or by any means without the prior written permission of the publisher, nor be otherwise circulated in any form of binding or cover other than that in which it is published and without a similar condition being imposed on the subsequent purchaser.

Fraser Beath McEwing
Why Does My Dog Bark
ISBN: 978-1-925707-56-4
pp286

About the Author

A writer and magazine editor for most of his career, Fraser Beath McEwing has been published in many leading Australian magazines and newspapers.

His experience in the Melbourne textile industry led him to become managing editor of Rupert Murdoch's *Australian Fashion News*. In 1972, he founded his own Australian fortnightly fashion industry newspaper, *Ragtrader*, and ran it for 20 years.

Fraser Beath McEwing is also a fiction writer. His first novel, *Feel the Width,* was published in 1994. It took a satirical look at the Australian fashion industry of the 1960s. His experience in the early 1990s with network marketing formed the basis of his second satirical novel, *cafe*. His current trilogy, Adam Exx, delves into speculative fiction.

In addition to being a writer, Fraser has been a textile wholesaler, furniture importer and retailer, a champion squash player, a competition tennis player and a pianist. From 2012 he became a classical music concert reviewer for the Sydney Symphony Orchestra, and has built up a wide audience. He is a board member of the Theme & Variations Foundation that assists young Australian pianists achieve their goals.

Also by Fraser Beath McEwing

Feel the width
Cafe
Adam Exx Book 1 Genesis
Adam Exx Book 2 Exodus
Adam Exx Book 3 Leviticus

Acknowledgements

I am most grateful to the people who read the early manuscript and offered comment. They include, but are not limited to, Jocelyn Walker, Michelle McEwing, Samuel Leon, Harvey Little. And special thanks to Ivo Porfiri who read and debated many of my conclusions about religion; to Ross Terrill, highly successful writer and Harvard professor who encouraged me; to Ray Stewart, who applied his literary and editing talents to the manuscript many times over.

And thank you to the many unnamed people who assisted, even though they would not have been aware of it. Casual conversations about the subject matter often yielded valuable points of view that I either embraced or used as confirmation of my own findings.

Foreword

Why does my dog bark? Off-the-cuff answer: because it's a dog. Correct answer: because Mind Architecture governs its behaviour, and that compels it to bark. Dogs have Mind Architecture specific to their species. So do we — but thankfully ours doesn't oblige us to bark. Welcome to what makes humans tick.

As you can see, this is not a long book, although it could have been. Maybe it should have been. If I had set out to write a scholarly work, I would have needed far more examples, quotations, facts and footnotes to back up my conclusions. But even then, there would have been plenty of contrary opinions. There will be anyway, no matter how these ideas are presented. And that's good. This subject deserves debate.

I'm sure you feel as irritated as I do when a solution to an everyday problem is offered on the internet, and we have to watch half an hour or more of tedious detail before we're told what the solution is and how much it will cost. Some lifestyle books are like that too. They labour the point so much that it gets lost in the tangle of minutia. I wanted to avoid that. I've been brief and I don't apologise for it.

This book will never be finished — not by me, anyway. After the first draft, I thought, that will do. I have enough examples to make the point that we are a product of, and are bound by, Mind Architecture. But, like knowledge itself, the end kept moving away from me. I'd think of another component of Mind Architecture that just had to go in, forcing me to reopen the file. Eventually, I had to accept the fact that I would probably never unearth all the components. I felt like a palaeontologist, knowing there are more treasures to be found, but having to leave the dig for others to continue — if they are interested.

One way this topic could have been approached would have been to compare our minds and thought processes to those of other living creatures to show where we differ. But that would have missed the central premise of what I wanted to do: to distil why humans behave the way they do. Having said that, I have used a few comparisons for illustration, and to show that we are arguably at the top of the earthly assembly of living creatures, although I am certain, albeit we can't yet prove it, that on a universal scale we're well down in the mind attainment stakes.

Foreword

During the billions of years that life could have existed, it is hard to believe that we rank number one.

Publishers, book shops and libraries categorise books by genre. This makes sense for both buyers and sellers. But many books, especially those found on the lifestyle and self-help shelves, fit into more than one category. Lifestyle and self-help can delve into philosophy, practical problem solving or explore a subject to which an author believes he or she has something to add. This book is one of those that fits into more than one category.

While being aware of the existence of Mind Architecture is interesting in itself — maybe even astonishing to some — it is the application of the knowledge that can bring many additional benefits. While Mind Architecture dominates, or at least constrains our behaviour, there are escape routes, some of them temporary and others worth striving for as permanent.

One of the most beneficial applications of understanding Mind Architecture comes under the heading of 'conscious suspension'. If we can analyse and categorise components of Mind Architecture, we can then see what we have to work with to make our lives better.

Contents

About the Author		iii
Acknowledgements		v
Foreword		1
Contents		5
Chapter 1	The Source	7
Chapter 2	What is Mind Architecture?	21
Chapter 3	Hierarchies	31
Chapter 4	Size	47
Chapter 5	Comparisons	53
Chapter 6	Crime and Punishment	63
Chapter 7	War and Peace	73
Chapter 8	Life and Death	83
Chapter 9	Love	89
Chapter 10	Artistry	99
Chapter 11	Time	103
Chapter 12	Change	109
Chapter 13	Obstacles Create Happiness	119
Chapter 14	Blame	137
Chapter 15	Belief	141

Chapter 16	Anger and Fear	149
Chapter 17	Questioning	157
Chapter 18	Addiction	161
Chapter 19	Revenge and Forgiveness	165
Chapter 20	Guilt and Remorse	171
Chapter 21	Luck	177
Chapter 22	Ownership	181
Chapter 23	Ritual and Symbol	187
Chapter 24	Imagination	193
Chapter 25	Expectation	199
Chapter 26	Dressing	203
Chapter 27	Networking	207
Chapter 28	Systems	211
Chapter 29	Uniqueness	217
Chapter 30	Enough is Enough	221
Chapter 31	The Pied Piper of Technology	227
Chapter 32	MA and the Future	249
Chapter 33	Applying the Knowledge	255

CHAPTER 1

The Source

I can't tell you exactly where this book came from, but I can tell you how it came about.

In 1992, my wife Michelle and I decided to leave Australia for a year to travel the world. I'd sold my publishing company and I was trying to decide what to do with the rest of my life. When most of my friends left school, they took the obligatory sea trip to England, stayed in Earl's Court and lived in the style of the satirical cartoon character, Barry McKenzie. But I'd gone straight from school to work and part-time university. I had never taken the youthful, overseas adventure. I felt somehow owed. Payback was my wife and I buying two around-the-world tickets from KLM Airlines that allowed us, over a period of twelve months, many stopovers which we could nominate as we went along. I regarded the year we spent wandering around Europe as our gap year, except that it was not a breather before university enrolment, but a breather before re-enrolling in Australian life.

Although I love writing travelogues, the 1992 trip narrative is another story for another time — except what happened at the very beginning. We made our first stop in Los Angeles. There were quite a few reasons for this, but two of mine were to buy a Macintosh portable computer, then unavailable in Australia, and to attend a seminar by a channelled entity called Lazaris.

I'd come across Lazaris when a friend gave me a tape in which a man with an unfathomable accent talked about creating abundance and our own reality. While his ideas were interesting, and ultimately difficult to implement, the method of delivery aroused my curiosity. An apparently unremarkable American man called Jach Pursel was running seminars in which he channelled, to use his words, a 'multi-levelled consciousness that was simultaneously aware of many different, nonphysical realities'.

While I never became an ardent follower of Lazaris, I did subsequently write a story for *The Australian Women's Weekly* recounting my experience of the seminar and discussing the authenticity of channelling. There was quite a reaction to the article. Some readers wrote in suggesting that dark forces had taken hold of me and that I should seek help from a minister of religion. In the ensuing years, Jach's channelling of Lazaris has endured, creating a sizeable number of believers — along with some sceptics who claim the whole idea is a scam. I'm not comfortable on either side, although I will say that nobody has yet proven Lazaris to be a scam and Jach doesn't seem to have grown rich on the proceeds of selling Lazaris material.

The veracity of Lazaris is not the issue here, but channelling is. What Lazaris did for me was point me towards considering the practical application of channelling, and I don't mean the kind where a spooky medium, sitting in a darkened room, brings messages from the dead. That is really open to suspicion. The kind of channelling I'm talking about is common to most people when they search within themselves for words or ideas or solutions that don't seem to exist in their conscious minds and are often beyond their estimated capability. They often explain a breakthrough as 'it just came to me'.

My personal and continuing experience of channelling comes largely through writing, mostly centred on journalism and fiction. Early in my career, I learned to rely on 'the channel' to produce written material that seemed to go beyond my conscious ability — although I hadn't yet identified it as such. I'm certain that all successful journalists do something similar. They've done the interview or assembled the facts and now they sit down at a keyboard to write the story. They may be unaware that they've slipped into channelling mode, preferring to explain their ability to write as a gift, or knack or something that's based on many years of experience, and therefore largely mechanical.

In fiction writing, channelling is even more necessary than in journalism. Creating characters, events and locations calls for extraordinary free-range thought that needs to roam outside the boundaries of the familiar. I'll accept that maybe we're tapping into our subconscious, because I'm ambivalent about the existence of a new age spirit world. I simply don't know where the channel is located, but I am convinced of its existence. There is no other explanation for the material in this book that, in turn, owes its existence to my *Adam Exx* fiction trilogy, which was a product entirely of imagination.

Channelling is most obvious in the arts where a brilliant outcome will often surprise the artist, although he or she may refuse to acknowledge that the creative inspiration was a mystery, since it may dilute the adulation due to the artist who produced the work. My wife's mother, who was quite a successful Australian working artist, did not believe in new age spiritualism, nor was she religious and she certainly held no optimism for an afterlife. Yet when she stood before a new white canvas and lifted her brush, she was quite happy to acknowledge that the paint and strokes she put down were being supplied and guided by something outside of herself. When I suggested to her that this was channelling, she agreed that was one way of describing her creative experience.

Channelling is less obvious in other fields like business, technology or science. But that doesn't mean it isn't part of the creative process. Granted, these endeavours have more practical, measurable outcomes, which may mask their esoteric connections. It is generally acknowledged that Einstein's ground-breaking theories of relativity were not the end result of a long build-up of mathematical and physics formulae, but a difficult-to-explain leap from what he knew to what he produced. This gap is clearly a channel at work. This is how Einstein explained channelling, without identifying it as such:

> 'The intellect has little to do on the road to discovery. There comes a leap in consciousness, call it Intuition or what you will, the solution comes to you and you don't know how or why.'

There have been many other scientific breakthroughs showing a similar progression, with an inexplicable gap before the eureka discovery. Granted, an inventor may have the ingredients and training at his disposal, but it is his channel that places them in a new sequence to create the discovery.

In my experience, the channel can make a contribution at virtually any time. People, such as writers or composers, can turn on the channel almost at will — as I am doing writing this book. But the channel can also spring a surprise. It can deposit an idea or a solution at the moment of waking from sleep. When that happens to me, I jump out of bed and write it down because there is every chance that, if I allow myself to doze, it will be gone the next time I wake. I've also found that the channel can deliver an idea when my mind slips into neutral, such as during a gym workout. My most productive time is when I'm lying on the floor, my legs resting on an exercise ball and I'm simply letting my back relax flat against the mat. I often get up with a good, but unbidden idea.

Maybe the dream state and the exercise state cause our conscious mind, which is usually buzzing away on any number of thoughts, to give the channel some space to bring us an idea. Everybody is different as to when they can best let their channel in. It is worth doing a little personal research to discover yours.

This is not to say that the channel is always correct. In

CHAPTER 1 The Source

fact, it is fallible, when you think of the many people who once believed pronouncements from their priests who intimidated scientists into declaring that the earth was flat, or that the Earth was the centre of the universe and didn't orbit the sun. In less lofty examples we see people acting in the belief that they are following some out-of-body instructions. Other people hear voices, some telling them to commit crimes. We must be careful not to mix channelling with mental disorders - although the two are sometimes linked.

If we accept that the channel is fallible then, perhaps, we can take it out of always-right spiritual hands and make it part of us, where we acknowledge imperfection.

It will become obvious later why I'm making a case for personal channelling. It was the conduit that enabled me to write about Mind Architecture when, in fact, I had little prior knowledge of what I was writing about or even the intention to pursue it. In the process of writing three speculative fiction novels, I put my main character into a position where he needed to call on his channel — which really meant that I had to call on mine. I could have avoided having to deal with his by stepping around it in the plot, but I handed it over to my channel — as I usually do when I have to write something — and it delivered. The story continued to the conclusion I wanted and the trilogy was finished. But when I looked back on it, I realised that it had revealed something far greater than what was needed for the story. Laid out before me was what really governs our behaviour. It explained what we are. My channel gave it the name Mind Architecture.

Although I run the risk of some spoiling for people who will read the trilogy, it is necessary to run over the story's outline. My main character, Adam, is the first man on Earth but living in contemporary Sydney. Adam finds himself, in book three, to be the only human left in existence. Humans have been created as an experiment and allowed to naturally develop, under observation. The rest of humanity has been wiped out and Adam pleads with his creators to reinstate humans, recreate planet Earth as they knew it, and let them go on developing. The creators eventually agree, but on the condition that Adam provides the fundamentals that go to make up the human mind and its workings. This is, in reality, the creators testing Adam. It forces him (and therefore me) to think of himself and his behaviour, along with all the people he has known throughout his life, objectively instead of subjectively. He has to decide what makes us human in such a way as to enable the creators to follow his findings if they are to achieve reinstatement.

The challenge he faces, and we all face when problem solving, is to disengage from our personal involvement

CHAPTER 1 The Source

and simply work with the facts. Judges are supposed to do this in legal determinations. And, as we know, it is not easy for them to disengage from their own life experiences. Adam is similarly challenged. He (aka me) is called upon to step out of his human shell to look dispassionately at what humans are, and therefore what determines our behaviour.

In the story, Adam gets help from the use of a relatively mild psychotropic drug. But because I was the puppet master, and didn't want to go down the drug path, I used my channel to create the story solution. As far as the drug is concerned, here's an extract from *Book 3 Adam Exx Leviticus*:

> SE Twelve came out of her cubicle when she heard me arrive. 'I think we've got the name of what we want. It's actually a light anaesthetic drug, which blocks pain and brings the subconscious to the surface. The patient is fully awake but uninhibited. It is called 'Airlift Eight Nine,' and is pretty common in hospitals.'

In Adam's case, the use of the drug, along with some searching questions, result in the revelation of Mind Architecture (from hereon, I'll simply call it MA), which was, in fact, supplied by my channel. After it had served its purpose in the book, I lifted it out as a stand-alone concept: the book you are reading now. Again, I've used my channel to add to it along the way.

That's what this book is about: identifying MA and the components that make it up. It is also about the role that channelling plays in producing ideas and conclusions that go beyond what appears to be the limitations of conscious knowledge or reasoning.

You won't find all the components of MA set down in these pages. At some point I had to call time and finish writing. The channel will no doubt supply me with more, and I'll wish I had waited a little longer to include them. You will probably devise some additions too, whether through your conscious observations of human behaviour or by using your own channel. So, we are entering a partnership. Just as science has now mapped the physical human genome, we are mapping human behaviour determined by MA.

And what is the use of such a map? As you'll see when we get into behaviour categories, there is one that stands out. It is our ability to suspend them for a limited time. Once we understand what we are made of mentally, and we can label those components, we can switch them off for a while. On an individual level, MA can help us to understand our friends and especially our enemies, and to anticipate their actions because, whether they like it or not, they are all irrevocably locked into MA. Those who understand its operation and presence are in a more powerful position than those who don't. You may become a little more sympathetic to what you see as human failings when you realise that we are confined within MA — as is every living creature. Each has its own MA, and they all differ between species.

It is worth digressing here to talk a little more about channelling. Everybody uses it to a greater or lesser degree. We have all experienced breakthrough solutions when trying to overcome a problem or a challenge. At those times, we've probably plugged into our channel without realising it. People whose careers depend directly upon frequent creativity are more habitual channel-users. For many of them, like me, it turns on automatically. Very few, however, recognise it as channelling. They see the results as simply the surfacing of good ideas that got them to the finish line.

Like driving a car, channelling becomes virtually involuntary over time, but there are ways to switch it on when needed — especially if you've never been consciously aware of its existence or you want to make more use of it.

The channel works in three modes. The first is the 'applied' channel, in which we combine it with conscious knowledge and methodology to produce practical solutions. That is what I'm doing right now. I know the English language and the rules of grammar, I have knowledge of the subject, and I have a book-writing task on the go. I invoke the channel by allowing it. Because the channel is very much part of us and is always prepared for action, all we need to do is invite it in and it will start to work for us — at its own pace.

The second mode is 'remote'. Let's say we're not sitting, grinding our teeth as we search for an urgent solution to a problem, but we know one will eventually be required. In this mode, we simply and clearly set the problem out in our mind, or we might discuss it with a friend — but then we stop thinking about it. The solution will arrive when least expected. Maybe we are taking a shower, or playing golf or gardening or washing up. Suddenly the channel will deliver. We must be ready for it.

It is worth becoming familiar with how your channel works and exercise it. In that way it can become a practical or even life-changing tool.

The third channelling mode is 'automatic'. It is used by MA to send all living creatures unbidden instructions. Some animals take life-preserving action that appears to be above their mental capacity or memory. Nobody has told them it's spooky or supernatural, so they just go ahead and do it. Migrating birds are a prime example. At a certain time in the year, they take to the air and, in some cases, fly vast distances to reproduce or feed. I doubt that a bird has the reasoning skills to work out why the taxing journey is necessary, or the ability to navigate, or calculate a flight — taking into account energy required and fuel load. While some birds perish on the migratory journey, most make it through. The only place a bird can get the instructions necessary to make a migratory flight is channelled automatically from its MA. The same principle applies to other animal behaviour. We usually put these kinds of feats down to that all-encompassing word 'instinct,' but it is obvious to me that they tap into their channels naturally.

Human MA has far fewer instructions channelled automatically than that of other living creatures. Our position at the top of Earth's cognitive ladder gives us more behavioural choice within each component of MA. Human channelling is more optional than it is with species lower down. If we never opted to use channelling, that would not be life-threatening, whereas if migratory birds were deprived of their channelled instruction to migrate, they probably wouldn't survive as a species.

This book is not about channelling, interesting as it is. The reason I've touched upon it is to explain why I, not being a behavioural scientist or a professor of anything, can claim to be an authority on MA. It simply began as my channel providing a solution to a fiction story problem, and then me using that solution, again with the help of my channel, to develop it into a stand-alone revelation.

CHAPTER 2

What is Mind Architecture?

*Architecture tends to consume everything else;
it has become one's entire life.*
Arne Jacobsen

Just as building architecture lays down a design to accommodate the function of a structure, MA lays down the design elements of our minds that direct our behaviour and make us what we are.

If an architect is asked to design a city office building, there is no point in drawing and specifying a football stadium. Every architectural project serves a purpose. Whether MA is created to produce a behaviour patten, outcome or we work back from our behaviour to define

MA as its source, is a moot point. It is a chicken and egg conundrum and the answer doesn't really matter. The fact is that they are both the product of each other.

The architecture of our minds serves the purpose of originating and managing our behaviour. It also conforms to our species, meaning that we are not as free as we'd like to think. The human mind is limited to, and by, its architecture — as is every species of living creature. They each have a different MA. The human one is the most complex — that we know of — but is highly likely exceeded elsewhere in the universe.

It is valid to ask, if there is architecture, who is the architect? The immediate answer from religious people is that the architect, not only of MA, but the entire universe, is God. As science probes the nature of the universe and theorises on its creation, the more awesome it appears and the more awesome the power of God appears. On the other side of the argument are scientific atheists who come up with opposing possibilities. There are those who say it all happened by chance, but that is difficult for us to appreciate because we're stuck in the middle of it and can't get outside to see it objectively. Others theorise that there are infinite universes and this just happens to be the one we're in — which includes MA. I don't have an issue with any of these explanations. I simply don't know, nor do I wrestle with the solution. What I do know is that MA exists and that it directs our behaviour.

It is also valid to ask whether we can use MA as an excuse for anti-social behaviour based on the premise that if we are not in control of our actions, then we can't be blamed for wrongdoing. Not so. We are in control of our actions, but within the confines of MA. There is no right or wrong in universal terms. Right and wrong, and the moral code that the majority of people aspire to for most of the time, has been devised by us within MA through all its components acting upon us all the time. Our human understanding of right and wrong, or success and failure, or nice and nasty, is entirely of our doing within the confines of MA. It doesn't necessarily apply anywhere else in the universe, or to any other species on Earth, for that matter. If we could speak the language of bees, for instance, we could thrust our heads into the hive and point out to the occupants the wrongs of inequality, where some bees work all day while others lie about gorging themselves and enjoying sex with the queen.

To quote from the Christian Bible, 2 Samuel 7:19: 'For my thoughts are not your thoughts, neither are your ways my ways, said the Lord.' Whether you believe the Bible was written by people or came from a deity, we are accepting that the way we see moral issues depends upon where we sit in the social spectrum and what species we belong to. Most animal groups would be appalled at the way our species wastes resources and how we kill for the sake of killing.

This is not a work of philosophy. I am not trying to understand or attempt to explain the 'why' of our existence, just the 'what'. MA is the 'what' that drives our behaviour.

We judge our worth by comparing our assets with those around us. But when it comes to human MA itself, the only living comparisons that can be made are with other creatures on Earth. Since we sit at the top of the intellectual ladder, we have yet to discover anything above us against which to measure human worth or be able to project where MA advancement might take us. Apart from animals, which we know we outthink, the only other avenue of comparison is with machines, which can be built to process information faster than we can mentally. However, machines are limited to the creative capabilities of those who build them: us. Although we are tantalised by the question as to whether machines will ever become self-aware and therefore rise above humans, there is no sign of this happening so far — in spite of some persuasive science fiction stories.

Let's forget about us for a while and look at dogs — which is where we came in. As we know, dogs come in all shapes and sizes. While we initially identify authentic dogs by their appearance, it takes their behaviour to convince us that we are experiencing real dogs. A statue or stuffed animal that looks like a dog is not a dog, and neither is a picture, or a movie depicting a dog. We are aware of the behaviour of dogs. They bark, wag their tails, and fetch. A dog does all of that because of its MA. It cannot do otherwise. It does not meow, purr or scratch adversaries. That's what cats do. While there is some common behaviour between dogs and cats, we don't have trouble identifying one from the other. But if we swapped their MAs, that would really confuse us. A barking, tail wagging cat? A purring, meowing, scratching dog? Whoa!

Of course, there are plenty of living creatures that demonstrate behaviour that might look as though they are borrowing from one another or imitating, but this is not really the case. There are limits to the components of MA — which have been evolved to suit our earthly environment. In terms of atoms, all living creatures are made of the same stuff. It is only atomic and then molecular combinations that make them different. MA works the same way. It differs for every category of living creature, including us, and determines behaviour within the design of the species. Dogs, cats and humans can all be identified as belonging to different species, each having a specific MA which determines behaviour. That is not to say living creatures within each species behave identically, but the amplitude of behavioural variation is both predictable and limited.

I explored the boundaries of that amplitude in my trilogy. There isn't a lot of sex in my *Adam Exx* books, but in Book 3 Adam is being questioned by a female that is actually a retail fashion mannequin come to life. Many men have seen a female mannequin in a store window when its outfit is being changed. For a moment, it stands there naked and they probably can't help noticing its slim, too-perfect body, long fingers, moulded hair, exquisite face. And they might question how they would feel if that were a live woman. Furthermore, how they would feel if she invited them for sex. They would be confused. She's real and unreal at the same time. Which belief would overcome the other? Adam faced this dilemma, with the added pressure that he hadn't had sex in a long time. I won't spoil the outcome for you, but there are valid arguments for both acceptance and rejection.

While all humans have very similar MAs, none are identical, just as no two people are physically identical. MA follows the rules of variety within species. MA is not linked to physical appearance. The components of MA are present in all of us, and they determine our behavioural patterns, given that they vary in intensity and in time frames. They are similar to variations in the human form: some tall, some short, some fat, some thin — but we acknowledge them all as people.

No matter what we do, our behaviour is confined within the boundaries of human MA. It is the force that pre-determines why we advance and regress as a species, why we fight, why we love and why we obey. It cannot be any other way — except for some escape hatches I've called Conscious Suspension in a later chapter.

That brings up the emotive word: freedom. Should we believe that MA deprives us of freedom? We often speak passionately about freedom of speech, of movement, of religion, of choice. We obviously value freedom, even though we are restrained by human-made laws and, below that in terms of severity, what society regards as acceptable behaviour. MA does not deprive us of freedom as long as it is within the shell of the architecture. Let me give you an example.

There is celebration at the zoo because a baby rhino has been born. From the baby rhino's point of view, the enclosure in which it now lives and what it can restrictively perceive beyond, is all there is. It can exercise choice within its zoo environment. It can run, lie down, swim in the pond and eat whenever it wants. The baby rhino doesn't know it is living in the artificial surroundings of a zoo and it exercises freedom to do whatever it likes within that environment. It doesn't contemplate escape because it is not aware of a place to escape to, or a reason to do so. The same cannot be said of its mother, who was captured in the wild and would probably like to get back there.

We are the equivalent of the baby rhino. We are confined within our Mind Architecture but because it is invisible, nor do we know what is outside it, we believe we can engage with freedom on any level our lifestyle allows. The prospect of our confinement within MA can upset people who believe in an unconfined spirit-world or a post-death existence in which MA does not exist.

There is quite a strong case to be made today that, in many affluent parts of the world, there is too much freedom. When we are so free that we can do virtually anything we like, freedom becomes a loss of direction.

Over the course of this book, I will briefly explore some of the major components of human MA. I don't pretend the list is exhaustive. You will probably think of other components until, like the completion of the human genome, we'll put it all together one day and have a complete, clear picture of why we behave the way we do.

A very important point I am about to make will crop up again, but I want to mention it here. One of the unique qualities of the human mind is that we can think about thinking. To me, that is quite remarkable and worthy of a thorough study. It may reveal not just two, but multiple minds present in our brains. But for now, let's settle for two. We can regard ourselves from outside ourselves. One of the popular tenets of most religions is to think 'pure' thoughts. The only way to do this is to direct our thoughts by thinking about them. That's pretty weird, but it exists, to the point where we've imitated it with self-repairing machines. Thinking about thinking doesn't appear to be shared with any other living creature on Earth — although we can't yet prove it.

The ability to control our thoughts gives us a spinoff in MA. Even though we are both enabled and limited by the components of our MA, because we can direct our thinking, we have the ability to suspend selected components of MA — for a while, at least. This overriding capability of human MA offers us some control over it, and goes to the usefulness of this book. Once we understand the components that make up MA, we have a chance to consciously suspend some of them — to our personal advantage or the common good.

Let's make a start in identifying the components of MA.

CHAPTER 3

Hierarchies

We cling to hierarchies because our place in a hierarchy is, rightly or wrongly, a major indicator of our social worth.

Harold Leavitt

While a triangle has many different meanings and serves many different functions, it also symbolises one of the most important components of MA. It doesn't matter whether it is a tall, skinny triangle or a low, squat one, but to understand how it applies to MA, it must be sitting with its base on the horizontal axis.

In the MA context, triangles illustrate hierarchy, which is the method of organisation that is fundamental to how we behave. We share this with many life forms on Earth, but let's discuss humans for the time being.

When there are two or more people in one location, they will form hierarchies. The more people, the bigger and more complex the hierarchies. Of course, it makes sense. In order for a group to survive, the bodily strong will head the hierarchy where physical power is required. The clever will head the hierarchy where problem solving is required. And the cunning, who may not be superior in any department, may get to the top of the hierarchy via a skill we recognise as politics.

Hierarchies are subject to cycles. They usually begin in chaos and finish with disintegration. They each have a time limit based on a mix of life expectancy, dedication and natural degradation of the participants. Some hierarchies, such as religions, might seem to continue unabated, but in fact they evolve and change as their constituents come and go.

Hierarchies are so common and so natural to us that we seldom stop to query or even acknowledge their presence. We just accept them as the way things are — and have to be. Charles Darwin's *On the Origin of Species*, simply took the dynamic of triangular arrangements and postulated that those on top lived while those at the bottom died via 'natural selection', with the corollary that those at the top won better reproductive opportunities for themselves so that their offspring inherited abilities that those further down didn't. Thus, the species evolved towards greater strength and improved its chances of survival against opposing external forces.

In a chicken and egg question we might ask whether hierarchies produce leaders or leaders produce hierarchies. And like the chicken and egg, both are true. If a great leader rises up with an idea that people want to follow, a hierarchy will form beneath him or her. And if a movement starts out of consensus, (such as the belief in man-made climate change,) it will create spaces for leaders. Either way, leadership and hierarchies are two sides of the one coin. They produce our heroes. They also create sub-leadership spaces all the way down the triangle. The people that fill the spaces are not always either competent or the best choice for the job, so in most hierarchies there is continuous reshuffling.

If we are looking at the top of the pyramid of a typical human hierarchy, we see that the success of the leader depends upon the qualities of his or her leadership, the timing of his or her reign, the degree of need for his or her leadership and the fit of qualification to the role. If I stood up and proclaimed myself leader of people who want to scratch their left armpit every Thursday afternoon at precisely 3.04 pm, I wouldn't have any followers. No hierarchy exists for that activity, so my proposed leadership does not lead anybody and therefore I am not a leader. Hierarchies can only exist when there is a consensus for a cause to be pursued.

All our institutions, companies and organisations are built on hierarchies. The armed forces, governments at all levels, big and small businesses, clubs, teams, religious bodies — all hierarchies. If we form a club, we need a president, a secretary and a treasurer — which we duly elect. When we meet formally, we follow an approximately triangular arrangement. And we do not question this. It's how to properly organise a group that has a common purpose. How else could you do it? No other system has yet replaced it. Why? Because MA has determined that this is how we must behave. It is one of the most powerful components of MA, illustrated by the universal acceptance and need for hierarchies.

Of course, there are short-lived exceptions. There will always be somebody who tries resisting hierarchies and will suggest, or even put into practice, an alternative system, but they never survive. And let's not forget the person who pretends to be from low down in a hierarchy but is really from higher up and can return there at will. Typical of this is a show on television called *Undercover Boss*. There are many reasons why people play this game, not all of them admirable.

CHAPTER 3 Hierarchies

With the threat of overpopulation leading to serious damage to Earth's eco-system, we might conclude that we've survived too well and haven't allowed naturally occurring hierarchies to sort us out. It is possible that wars and natural disasters are both desirable and necessary to slow us down and cull our numbers. Still in Darwinian mode, we might also recognise that we are currently opposing the survival of the fittest by protecting the weakest for so-called moral reasons, along with attempting to maintain the existence of other species threatened with extinction. While this may satisfy our collective conscience, it interferes with what we accept as Darwinian natural law — which is another way of saying hierarchies. What the consequences of this will be can only be guessed at.

Some years ago, when Australia still manufactured most of its clothing (because the factories were protected by severe import restrictions) as a journalist I interviewed a factory owner who wanted to break down the hierarchy of boss and workers. He offered his employees the opportunity to run the factory on consensus. Every decision that had to be made was made by the whole staff in which all opinions were heard and votes taken. As well as an interesting social experiment, it turned into a grim comedy. Hours were spent in meetings rather than sewing. The factory became so chaotic and inefficient that the business went broke. Everybody involved in the experiment thought they wanted autonomy and cooperation, but their MAs disagreed and, of course, MA prevailed.

Politically, the world's governmental systems are roughly divided between dictatorship and democracy, with many layers in between. Those who are proud of their democratic government may say that it runs counter to a dictatorship because almost anybody can stand for parliament and everybody's vote counts equally. But further examination shows this as simply reinforcing our underlying belief in hierarchies because we cast our votes to create them. Democracy goes out the window once the votes are counted.

Communism, in its purest form, resists hierarchies but it begins to become polluted from the moment it is set up because everybody involved in the movement is obliged to adopt hierarchies according to their inescapable MA.

Hierarchies are not separated or neatly spaced out in our behavioural map. Nor are they static. All of us are part of multiple hierarchies that are forever growing, shrinking and distorting — almost like miniature cosmoses. We can be high in one and low in another, but that is not the gauge of our level of satisfaction with our position. It is much more to do with where we want to be, compared with where we really are. In an upcoming chapter we will be dealing with comparisons as a component of MA. Comparisons play a role in hierarchies because they determine our assessment as to how happy we are with our position and may motivate us to try to climb higher or become disenchanted and leave the hierarchy altogether.

Nowhere is an MA hierarchy more clearly illustrated than in religion. A typical religion has a deity at the top of the triangle from whence 'irrefutable' truths and behavioural instructions are given to a prophet, who then passes on the deity's message to the laity. To this fundamental structure we have added an enormous number of variations, with rituals, taboos, deprivations, punishments and promises of an afterlife for the faithful. The deity's alleged original message can then become so distorted and weighed down by man-made extras that it gets lost in the embellishments. Religions are in competition with one another, each claiming to be the true path to enlightenment and grace. Logic tells us that they can't all be right, and the ensuing conflict over their differences has cost the human race dearly — and will continue to do so. But before we become too cynical about sometimes violently opposing organised religions, we should remember that conflict (in a later chapter) is another unavoidable MA component.

Considered as a whole, MA is not a cosy set of parallel components created for us by a deity or delivered benevolently by evolution. Many of them clash and, in doing so, give us opposing choices, but remain within the framework of MA. This is what makes us human.

Religions rise and fall in intensity over time. They are continually evolving, splitting, breaking away, speeding up and slowing down. Our compelling need for religious hierarchies leaves us susceptible to being duped and dominated by religious operators, in most cases clergy, who are themselves caught up in the need for hierarchy, but can also be corrupted by other demands of MA. They use the hierarchical system to further their own ambitions. Most members of the clergy walk the dual paths of religious calling and career. They are therefore in a continual state of confusion, steadfast as they may appear to the casual observer.

If there is such a thing as a deity in control of the universe, I doubt that it is anything like us and is completely beyond our current understanding. Unfortunately, also part of our MA, is a requirement to explain everything, even if it is way beyond our understanding. That is one part of MA I'd like to suspend. We must accept that we can't know everything, that knowledge accumulates over time, and will be continually proved and disproved.

Because there is no scientific evidence of a deity, MA dictates that we invent one. Historically, humans have tended to worship what they don't understand. At one stage it was the sun — but now that most of us understand the sun, it misses out on worship. Deities are much more useful. They are regarded as elusive, unknowable, unpredictable, infinitely powerful and open to interpretation. Occasionally, when a person claims to have had communication with a deity, and they report it convincingly enough, they can attract an enormous following. The great prophets of history are in this category.

If we don't understand creation, then we can still sleep soundly by handing it all over to the deity. The fact that astrophysics and religion are drawing further apart on the question of creation is a growing dichotomy. In the past, religions have been able to persecute those who have disagreed with them, sometimes by citing unspecified scientific grounds based entirely on faith. That still goes on today, although it is greatly diminished as science comes up with explanations that religions cannot match, forcing them either into successive fall-back positions or calling on adherents to shut out science and accept supernatural explanations without question.

In this discussion we should consider the roles of atheists and agnostics.

Atheists throw up some interesting questions in relation

to MA. There is some disagreement over the definition of atheism. One definition says that atheists believe there is no god while the other says that atheists do not believe in God. The difference, it must be said, is marginal. To fulfil their obligation to MA they presumably place their need for belief elsewhere.

Here is a quote from an essay by atheist, Adam Lee, who wrote the book *Daylight Atheism*. He is defending the accusation that atheists are arrogant.

> This argument holds that atheism springs from an arrogant desire for human independence, a desire to live without controlling authority or guidance. However, such a description could not be farther from the truth. Though I have known many atheists, I have never once met one who wanted to live free of all moral restraint or 'do his own thing' without any input from others. Just like everyone else, atheists recognise that there will always be those who are more intelligent than they, and are grateful to the wisdom of the teachers and mentors who guided them through life in the past and continue to do so. Just like everyone else, atheists recognise that rules of social conduct are necessary to create and sustain an orderly and harmonious society. We are fully aware of the necessity of accepting guidance and submitting to authority; we merely see no

evidence for the existence of a being called God that has any part to play in this process. Again, atheists are not motivated by perverse or selfish desire to reject the authority of a god whose existence they are fully aware of — rather, atheists are motivated by honestly held conviction that there is no good evidence for the existence of such an authority, and so it is up to us to figure out how to live together.

If atheists say there is no god, this appears to go against the MA dictum for a deity-based hierarchy. But in all probability, many of them substitute the existence of the universe, or a belief in orderly behaviour, in place of a deity. The fact that the universe exists means that there is some sort of creative force behind it, otherwise it wouldn't be here and neither would we. Something caused it. But we are as yet unable to explain what that something is. To the atheist, the religion-backed idea of a deity is not acceptable. However, if we follow the debates between religious leaders and the likes of leading atheists Richard Dawkins and Christopher Hitchens, we will see that they clash mostly over the processes, procedures and effects of religion rather than the fundamental question of deity because neither side can make a provable case. 'How do you know there is a god?' is equally countered by 'how do you know there isn't?' The religious affiliates have created a god in their own image (and then tell us, with no evidence, that we are created in God's image) and then use God as a receptacle to contain matters that cannot be explained scientifically. But nobody, to my knowledge, has come up with the explanation that deities or their substitutes are irresistible because MA forces hierarchies upon us.

Agnostics are fence sitters, and probably account for the majority of opinion on religion — although few people are inclined to label themselves as agnostics. An agnostic is defined by the Merriam-Webster Dictionary as: 'a person who holds the view that any ultimate reality (such as God) is unknown and probably unknowable: one who is not committed to believing in either the existence or the nonexistence of God or a god.' Whereas atheism involves what a person does or does not believe, agnosticism involves what a person does or does not know. Belief and knowledge are related but nevertheless separate issues.

Shedding some light on all this is a consideration of the solitary person. That changes the application of MA. Much of it lies dormant, because MA only fully comes into play where there is more than one person involved. However, the subject we've just been discussing, deities and religion, can apply just as much to the solitary person as it does to the crowd. This is because MA is in the mind before it becomes actioned — and not all of it reaches the action stage. Religious deities can be accepted without ever being articulated. Our solitary person can, and probably will, create some kind of deity-based system in his mind. This might be to explain his environment where he has no acceptable scientific answers to naturally occurring questions. We will revisit the solitary person when we come to discuss laws in a later chapter.

While we're on the subject of religious deities, it is worth mentioning the role of prayer that MA has programmed into us. Prayer is common to virtually all religions and, largely because of this, has earned general respect, despite doctrinal differences. Adherents ask the deity, with or without the use of the voice, to act on their behalf. While prayer can be used to praise the deity and give thanks for what has been bestowed either by the deity or other benefactors, a great deal of it is directed towards a particular outcome that the praying person wants — and not necessarily for his or her personal benefit. One fundamental problem with prayer is that it often seeks the deity's intervention in a future sequence of events, but those doing the asking can have opposing requests. While this poses a theoretical problem for the deity it poses a greater practical problem for those praying. Those who receive a favourable outcome can claim that prayer worked whereas those on the losing side have to console themselves with the proposition that the deity did what was best, although it didn't seem so at the time. This begs the question that if the deity always decides outcomes, why pray at all, except to give praise, which religious cynics see as keeping up insurance payments.

Apart for asking for the deity's intervention in current and future events, a great deal of prayer is directed towards praising the deity. Giving thanks for what we have soon becomes an outpouring of telling the deity, using every praiseworthy superlative in the language to express what a magnificent entity the deity is. There is no evidence that the deity wants, likes, or even acknowledges these lashings of praise. MA dictates that we make the assumption that our praising prayer is being received and enjoyed by the deity. This is purely based on the effect of similar outpourings among ourselves. Because we lap up praise, we assume the deity does too.

I am not intending here to be disrespectful to prayer but rather to look at it dispassionately. It is so universal and deep-seated in our human psyche, and so many worthy people use it and believe in it that it must be regarded as an essential part of human behaviour. We need prayer and there is no doubt that prayer has practical uses. It focuses the mind on pertinent issues and, like its non-religious counterpart, affirmations, it drives home resolves that the person praying is trying to attain. There are many forms of prayer that are not aimed at a religious figure like a deity or a saint. Reciting a resolve or belief in unison is a type of prayer. Talking to ourselves about the outcomes we want is another form of prayer. They all obey the process of 'putting requests and praise out there' through the voice or thought — so that the subconscious mind can get to work on a favourable outcome.

If we extend the concept of prayer beyond its use in religions, it becomes one of the most commonly used and powerful components of MA, and one we hesitate to mock. 'Hush! Hush! Whisper who dares! Christopher Robin is saying his prayers.' It is so widespread that we use it and accept it without question, even though there is no scientific evidence that prayer brings about change. Of course, if you repeat a prayer often enough there may be a perception of change, and earnest, fervent prayer may make the person doing the praying feel better, or perhaps satisfied that they have fulfilled a holy obligation.

Prayer generally doesn't do any harm and, in its many forms, comforts a huge number of people. But it is far from a supernatural phenomenon. Rather, it is an unavoidable and powerful component of MA.

Also, part of our MA's imposed sense of hierarchy is that of aspirations. In religion, we have created a hierarchy of behaviour where perfection is at the top and evil is at the bottom. We believe that we should always be trying to reach the top even though it cannot be reached. Knowing where and what the top is, provides us with a compass

— and MA urges us upwards. In all religions there exists upper levels of pious behaviour that barely allow time to have other life experiences. The reason why some people elevate themselves in the aspirational hierarchy is usually to get a reward in 'the next life'. And that's a bit risky because the current life may be all that there is.

There are many other MA based aspirational hierarchies. They can be found in virtually every field of human endeavour. We'll be dealing with laws in another chapter, but in terms of aspirational hierarchies the law is similar to religion in that we know what it is to be totally law abiding, but cannot reach the top. The same applies to sports, business, academia and music. Perfection is sitting up there beckoning us. We can see the path but can only climb so far.

CHAPTER 4

Size

*Size is nothing to the universe
(unlimited abundance if that's what you wish).
We make the rules on size and time.*
Rhonda Byrne

I love big questions, and none is bigger than: What size is the universe? The problem is that there is no fixed size because it is expanding. If you accept that it is about 13.8 billion years old, then light from the Big Bang will take 13.8 billion light years to reach us. But that doesn't allow for the expansion of the universe nor the probability that it is infinite. These questions and answers take us from our school ruler into theoretical physics. Granted, there are some fascinating answers, which are, themselves, rapidly being updated. The current real answer is that nobody is sure, and even if there were a definitive answer it would have no bearing on our cosmically brief lives — apart from an interesting piece of knowledge.

What does MA have to do with this? The answer is that MA comes with a built-in calculator. We estimate all sizes based on the human body. Our calculation of size, in its broadest meaning, includes everything we measure. If you want a neat package of size measurement, although it is only a tiny part of our total measurements, look at the Olympic Games. They tell us our size in many dimensions: how fast we can run, what weight we can lift, how high we can jump, plus all the variants when you add mechanical devices like bicycles, boats, balls and bars. The result is that we have a reference point for size relating to each of life's activities. If we live typically for seventy-five years, then we can use that as a comparative measure of time. We can place ourselves relative to all other living things, from insects that live for only one day to trees that live for thousands of years. From human statistics we form an opinion of the difference between a long and a short life.

We also use external indicators, especially for the passage of time. The behaviour of our solar system gives us reference points because it creates seasons which impact very directly on the way we live. But although these observable timekeepers seem to lead us, the truth is that we relate to them only through or own bodies and life expectancy. If our average life span were one second, then what the solar system was up to would be of little interest.

In my *Adam Exx* series, Adam requests his creators remake the known universe — which brings up the issue of how big it is. They solve the problem of it being too big, and taking too much energy to build, by shrinking it. As long as everything is shrunk in proportion, there is no perceived change.

Here is a practical example. The Eiffel Tower is 300 metres high and let's say a person observing it is two metres tall and is standing one kilometre from the tower. Pretend that the tower is not in the middle of Paris but isolated on a huge, concrete expanse that goes away forever on all sides. In other words, there are no distractions. Now, let's shrink the Eiffel Tower down to one metre tall. The observer can no longer see it unless we also shrink him or her and the distance from the tower by a proportionate amount. Then, to the observer, nothing has changed.

In essence, this was the solution Adam's creators came up with. If Adam returned to an earth the size of a tennis ball, compared to its current size, he would find no change as long as he had been shrunk by the same proportion.

So much for the story, but although it was fiction, it confirms that expressions of size amount to no more than the exercise of comparison — which is another of the components of MA and one of our limitations. We cannot comprehend absolutes in either direction. Science is confronted by the seemingly endless search for the dimensions of the universe on one hand and sub-atomic particles on the other. Both directions currently finish in the domain of theoretical physics because we hit the barrier of 'okay, but what comes after that?'

We are born with our MA irrevocably in place. It doesn't determine our physical development, or how long we will live, but obliges us, as humans, to have a relatively common comprehension of the world in which we find ourselves. If we can imagine the MA of a creature a billion light years in size with a life span a hundred million light years, the universe would appear quite different to the way it comprehends size and time. Coming at this another way, the MA of an ant is nothing like ours. Its universe is measured in tiny fractions compared to ours just as ours is measured in tiny fractions compared to the billion light years creature — which, incidentally, I am not suggesting exists.

All our so-called achievements and advancements have involved measurements, and those measurements all begin from looking at ourselves as the starting point. In a universal sense, there is no such thing as big or small, but only comparisons with ourselves.

CHAPTER 5

Comparisons

Alone, I am satisfied with myself. With others, I am beset by troubling comparisons.
Mason Cooley

There is an old saying: 'In the land of the blind, the man with one eye is king'. This neatly sums up another major component of MA. It is also present in the MA of many other living creatures. Basically, it says that we gauge our success in life not just by acquiring what we think we need or want, but by judging ourselves in the light of what other people have.

Comparisons with others' possessions, abilities and achievements become more important the closer they are to us. Thinking about the boy who came from the same socio-economic background as I did, I will feel happiness if I 'did better' than him or displeasure if I 'did worse'. We are not nearly so affected when we look at the wealthiest and most powerful people in the world. While we may want some or all of their power and riches, we don't generally beat ourselves up because we don't get them. Our reason for acceptance of remote wealth, power or ability — or our excuse for not reaching those heights — is that we can tell ourselves we didn't have the lucky 'right time, right place' break that they had.

As long as we accept that it was out of our control, we don't generally blame ourselves for failing to make it. God gave them better brains than ours, or they came from a richer family, or were born with more powerful bodies and there was nothing we could do about any of that. But achievement comparisons with our friends, relatives, co-workers, sporting opponents, club members — are all sitting there for our MA to process. While we may not like that part of our nature, we're stuck with it because it is part of our MA and therefore unavoidable.

One of the clearest examples of MA comparison in operation is when somebody asks us our age. There are exceptions, such as when an adult asks a child its age in polite conversation, or an official needs to know somebody's age for a documented record. MA comparison cuts in when one adult wants to know the age of another adult for no official reason. Immediately there is an assessment. What assets does he or she have in comparison to ours? If we are the same age, it is a clearer contest, but still abstractly scored in considerations of money, health, activities, reputation and community usefulness. Different assets will carry different values. If a different age, further allowances are made. A result is reached that we are pleased or disappointed with how we measure up in the comparison. If we're in negative territory that may encourage us to change our behaviour or simply remain disgruntled.

All people, from the most pious to the most sinful, judge themselves by comparison rather than if they have simply fulfilled their personal needs or personal potential. We often talk about these comparisons. We may praise high achievers for their feats but not always mean it, or we may discount what they have done because we don't match up. We live in a world of cross-comparisons and they drive many of our actions. Even though we have sufficient, we are pressed for more by MA — simply to improve our comparative position and therefore self-esteem.

One popular way of dealing with negative comparisons is to pull the other person down if we can't lift ourselves up. Most countries (Japan is an exception) are plagued by vandalism. One of the principal reasons given for this behaviour is socioeconomic disparity. The vandal, usually unconsciously, compares his position with that of higher achievers, in this case represented by a public train carriage and, by spraying graffiti or otherwise damaging its appearance, he brings the comparison with higher achievers a little closer to parity. Another type of vandalism is in publicly discounting the possessions, abilities and achievements of somebody we privately consider to be superior.

We spend time and energy trying to adjust our calculation of comparisons with others. The irony of this is that our view is exclusively personal. The view of others is certain to be different and, beyond that, the imaginary judgement of a deity.

There is a balancing factor in comparisons, which is worth noting. We are more likely to be kind to those we consider to be below us. A tendency toward balance is another part of MA — although we never achieve that balance for long because other factors in MA work against it, as we will see. But, like gravity, we are always aware of the pull towards balance. Ironically, in categories where we do approach balance, alarm bells start ringing and we move away from it by creating instabilities. These instabilities are, in turn, brought by another component of MA: change. Seemingly stable systems are always threatened by change, which may be quick or slow, but will always happen. I can't think of a single example of something that isn't subject to change. If the universe is subject to continual change, and we are part of the universe, then logically it applies to us too.

Kindness to those below us translates most obviously into charity, which manifests itself in a great number of ways, from donating to The Salvation Army to placing a coin in a beggar's cup or giving some money to a disadvantaged relative or friend. While we praise charity as virtuous, it is also an affirmation of where we see ourselves in the hierarchy of people. We are literally paying those who receive the benefit of our charity to remain in their place so that we can remain in ours. No charity ever elevates the recipient to a position above the giver.

Once again, this is not a judgement of good or evil, because there is no universal good or evil — which we'll deal with later — but simply identifying the working of MA.

Let's go a little further into MA applied comparisons. Everybody uses them. But there are as many ways of calculating them as there are people. While the principle of comparison (and it is not confined to humans) is universal because it is part of our MA, there is wide variation in how we formulate it and then what we do about improving it.

With comparison comes aggregation. We may feel okay

if we estimate our highs and lows as averaging above that of our peers. Each individual places an importance score on every one of life's assets. These scores are not numerical. They are notional and abstract, and they are subject to change. For example, let's say I'm a member of golf club and my handicap is twelve. I compare myself with players off scratch up to thirty-two. The comparison may be positive or negative just based on handicaps. But that won't be the case. The person on two used to be a pro and had years of doing nothing but play golf whereas my life was devoted to my work and family. Furthermore, I am wealthier than he, I am in better health and I am more popular at the club.

The aggregate of all those considerations may bring me to a positive comparison with the man who plays off two. But what about the player off twenty-nine? Certainly, I am the superior golfer but he is younger, has a wife that I am secretly attracted to, is a high-profile barrister and president of the club. The comparison with him could well turn out to be negative. It depends how much weight I give to each of his possessions, abilities and achievements to arrive at the aggregate. These calculations are seldom made in the conscious mind but are buzzing away in the subconscious all the time because we are always calculating our self-worth.

The way we calculate the value of the life assets that we

are using to compare to our own, is little understood. It cannot be measured by conventional means. It also varies between individuals who estimate assets differently. If you value money more than I do, then your comparison with another person's wealth will be different to mine and that may drive you to concentrate on the acquisition of wealth more than it will me. We have two types of measuring devices built into us. One operates externally, based on practicality and logic. We can weigh a bag of sugar and agree that it weighs one kilo. The other operates internally and subconsciously. Among many others, it runs physical calculations for us. When we are driving a car, it works out distance related to speed related to direction, and delivers the result to our handling of the car's controls. Not only that, but it continues to update us at computer speed. Calculations of this kind are innate and difficult to measure. The same goes for how we evaluate others' life assets for purposes of comparison to our own. All we know is that there are ongoing results in multiple departments that will either make us pleased or disappointed with ourselves. When we bundle all those departments together, we either feel good or bad about ourselves. And we know that this feeling can change quickly, depending upon what our aggregate comparison serves up to us.

Comparisons can be powerfully influenced by external persuasion. Wars break out over comparisons which have been packaged and presented by people or causes we believe in. The hierarchical structure that we spoke of earlier plays an important role here. People are nearly always led into war by those higher up in the triangle. The aggressors compare what they have with what they could have if they achieve a conquest. The defenders compare what they have with what they could lose if they are conquered. At the very beginning of a war the comparisons that both sides make is largely theoretical and often unreliable. And when it is over, the consequences are seldom what was anticipated.

Comparison has another side to it, too. MA has placed within us the fear that if we don't continually self-assess our position, we may lose what we've got, or fail to advance, or become depressed as we realise that some of our hopes and expectations can never be realised. Self-assessment brings and allows changes in our values. When we are young, physical prowess will be more value than it is when we're old. While we are competing in triathlons, we will be comparing our performance with those of other competitors, but when we're past being able to compete, self-assessment no longer places value on that activity. Wealth comes and goes in its value to us, too. Over time, our comparisons change and simplify, largely because they are age-based. Old people often feel happiness when they can to do things that people of the same age or younger cannot do.

CHAPTER 5 Comparisons

Although comparisons are most obvious on a personal level, there is a collective side to them. Right now, Australian educators are worried that our schoolchildren are not improving in their learning of the basics like language, maths and science which, after all, are the bones of learning. They are not saying that the unsatisfactory degree of learning achievement in these subjects will retard the advancement of the human race, but are basing their concern on comparisons with other countries. While not expressing it, there is an additional edge to their alarm because countries such as China, which used to be considered our intellectual inferior, have now surpassed us.

Something that I will repeat throughout the book is that we have the power to suspend many of our MA components. With effort, that can be for a long while, but the suspension requires continual work because MA drives us to conform to its structure. The real value of this book is that it doesn't only explain what MA is, but it gives us some ways to deal with it, even if we don't like it. This is where human MA differs from the MA of all other life forms on Earth. We alone can suspend some of its most powerful components — although not all. The behaviour of every other living creature is totally controlled by its MA and cannot be suspended — because no other living creature can comprehend MA.

CHAPTER 6

Crime and Punishment

As one reads history ... one is absolutely sickened, not by the crimes that the wicked have committed, but by the punishments that the good have inflicted.
Oscar Wilde

I'm not borrowing any more than the title of Dostoevsky's novel, although the story does illustrate another component of MA.

Let's visit that favourite character of mine: Solitary Man. He's sitting in his cave, having just captured, cooked and eaten a waterfowl along with some yams. Unfortunately, he has no way of making beer or wine, so he's had to wash down his dinner with a gourd of water from the nearby brook.

Solitary Man, or Sol as I'll call him, is a rare person on Earth who is not constrained by laws or penalties for breaking them. That is, with the exception of profoundly insane people to whom the law cannot apply. But if Sol walks down the coast far enough, he'll come upon civilisation and realise he is not alone. At that point MA will bury him in a behavioural avalanche. Part of that avalanche will be to do with laws, because wherever there is more than one person, MA dictates that laws will be created.

If Sol isn't constrained by laws and a whole lot of other behavioural patterns that make us what we are, we might ask whether Sol's MA is the same as ours. That uncovers one of the complexities of MA: It has latent sections that will only become operative if triggered by certain living conditions. People like Sol, who live abnormal lives compared to the vast majority, have only part of their MA operating. The same goes for insane people or those with afflictions that have stripped them of normality as accepted by the majority of people in a given time period. We could, of course, debate 'normality' but we'll save that for another time.

We make laws to direct behaviour by mutual consent. First and foremost, we want laws for our personal proection, to deter people from harming us. Laws are a trade-off. We agree to abide by a certain set of behaviours

CHAPTER 6 Crime and Punishment

as long as other people do the same. As a deterrent to disobeying this agreement we nominate penalties and create the means to enforce those penalties.

These are statute laws. But what about so-called moral laws that cover the exercise or failure to enact behaviours that show compassion, generosity and honesty — to name just some? Where do they come from? The same place that statute laws come from. The only difference is that they are not formalised and there are no penalties for breaking them. But they still emanate from our need for protection, in this case more hope than assumption. The golden rule: 'Do unto others as you would have them do unto you' sums up all laws, statute and moral. We swap some freedom of our own behaviour in return for a similar response from everybody else.

Here is a tantalising question: How many laws are there if we include all the laws of every country? I doubt that anybody has bothered to count them. Obviously, it would be a fearsomely difficult calculation with no obvious use for the answer. Moreover, it would never be finite because, during the counting, new laws would be enacted and some (a tiny few by comparison) would be repealed.

If you are tempted to take on this task, don't forget to include all criminal law, civil law and religious law. To that you ought to add lesser laws that are known by various names but let's call them rules and regulations. If there are no laws applying to Sol, we might ask why we, who live in communities, are so tightly laced with them? The answer is a sociological one bestowed upon us by MA. If we don't obey consensus-based behavioural patterns, then our chances of survival diminish to the point of annihilation. Take the simple example of road rules. Would you take your car out if there weren't hundreds of laws and rules that applied to everybody's driving? Even then, the road toll is an example of disobedience with terrible consequences.

While we might agree that laws are necessary for survival, they are primarily a part of MA. This becomes more evident if we look at animal behaviour. More primitive animals are motivated only by inherited and learned behaviour for their own survival. The interaction with others of their species is mainly to provide food, company and to reproduce. Unlike us, they have no awareness of laws that may never be applied to them.

As we move up in the intelligence chain, we find that animal communities seem to have laws, but again have evolved purely for survival. You could argue that our laws have also evolved for survival. Of course, some of them have, but a whole lot of others are not nearly so specific, with many based on preventing inconvenience, or modes of behaviour that simply annoy us.

CHAPTER 6 Crime and Punishment

Although we readily abandon systems that no longer apply, our laws can hang around long after they are usefully applicable.

Outdated Australian laws, but still on the statute books in various states, tell us it is illegal to go within one hundred metres of a whale carcass, interfere with a homing pigeon, vacuum a house between 10 pm and 7 am during weekdays, or have a lightbulb changed by anybody other than a qualified electrician. It is an offence to fly a kite 'to the annoyance of any person'. You can be jailed for cleaning up seabird or bat poo without a licence and you can also be fined thousands of dollars for possessing more than 50 kg of potatoes under certain circumstances. It is an offence to sing an 'obscene song or ballad' in a public place or to harness or attach your goat or your dog to a vehicle and drive it in or through a public area. Corresponding or doing business with pirates is illegal and can result in ten years jail. Hotels are required by law to stable, water and feed the horses of patrons. If you get electrocuted to death then you will have to pay fines to the government because, according Australian laws, it is illegal to touch electric wires that can lead to your death. The Vagrancy Act 1966 states it is against the law to pretend to tell people's fortunes — or use witchcraft or 'crafty science' for that matter — to discover where stolen goods might be found. In South Australia it is an offence to sell a refrigerator with a capacity of 42.5 litres or more, unless all of the doors can be easily opened from the inside or it was brought into the state before 1962.

That brings us to the other side of the law coin, punishment. In human terms, a statute law cannot exist unless there is punishment for breaking it. That punishment may not always be carried out, and occasionally there is punishment that is not in response to the breaking of a law, but every time a law is enacted, it is accompanied by prescribed penalties and punishments for breaking it.

Punishment is part deterrent for those contemplating breaking the law and part public revenge. Both these elements come from MA. While we might look upon the creation of laws and punishments as necessities to keep social order, they are, in fact, inescapable components of MA.

As humans, we have enlarged, enhanced and embellished the concept of laws and punishments. We now have laws ranging far beyond dealing with physical acts. Knowledge and intent are now being punished. A great deal of public energy goes into inventing laws, documenting them, enacting them and recording them — along with their corresponding punishments. Then we educate and employ vast numbers of people to interpret laws, apprehend offenders, build jails and execution equipment, and debate every link in this long chain. MA has seen to it that we are quite obsessed with laws. However, the vast numbers of laws that exist, with more being added continually, means that those who operate this gigantic law machine cannot possibly enforce even a fraction of the laws at their disposal. It is therefore left up to the detection and enforcement arm to decide which laws to pursue and which to ignore. Many laws are left on the statue books long after they have ceased to be enforced because public consensus no longer wants them, but can't be bothered repealing them. The fact that they are seldom formally abandoned is another part of MA, which dictates that laws will always grow in number but never diminish.

In summary, laws have not been invented only in the interests of orderly communal living, but are much more deeply rooted than that. They are a necessary component of MA. If we want to attribute the formation of MA to a deity, I won't argue with that, except to say that there are other possibilities.

Closely allied to crime and punishment, but not to be confused with them, are good and evil. To Sol, there is no good or evil behaviour, because they require the presence of others. Our laws are based around the prevention of evil, but not nearly so much the rewarding of good. For good, we rely on the judgement of others along with our personal estimation — which is based on the impact our 'good' has had on our own wellbeing and those with whom we've had direct or indirect contact. Good may be recognised in material gain, or words of praise and gratitude, or it may be simply self-satisfaction.

We don't get clear-cut slabs of what is good and evil from MA. What we do get is the ability to perceive majority attitudes to behaviour. Based on consensus, or 'community standards' good and evil ebb and flow. What was considered good at one time period can be regarded as evil in another. In the first half of the twentieth century it was considered 'good' to remove severely disadvantaged Australian aboriginal children from their families and bring them up in foster homes or institutions. But early in the twenty-first century this had switched to evil — prompting the Prime Minister to make a public apology to all Australian Aborigines on behalf of all non-Indigenous Australians on 13th February 2008. Likewise, what is regarded as good or evil can differ in many parts of the world at the same time. In Indonesia, sodomy is against the law and branded as evil, yet today in Australia it is accepted as okay, even normal, between consenting adults. Wars are fought over the evil that one side sees in the other.

It must be said that we conform to majority attitudes very loosely because the attitudes themselves are in a continuing state of disruption. While laws define what we will be punished for doing or not doing, there are many modes of behaviour which are not on the statute books, yet are regarded as mildly evil or socially unacceptable. An example might be farting in a crowded elevator or misbehaving in the workplace, which are not illegal but regarded as mildly evil.

Organisations like companies or institutions are participating more in punishing people who refuse to obey regulations specific to their neck of the woods. Recently I heard of a couple who were ordered off a flight in New Zealand because they refused to pay attention to the brief safety demonstration that every airline undertakes at the beginning of every flight. Without taking out my magnifying glass to read the terms and conditions that all airline travellers agree to when purchasing a ticket, I'm sure that paying attention to safety regulations would be covered, along with the acceptance that the airline can throw you off a flight for whatever reason it likes. Because it happens so rarely, few people think about it, any more than airlines point it out.

MA gives us the ability to read community attitudes so we can make a choice whether to heed them or not. If we decide against adherence, then we can assess the cost. Every protest marcher or meeting heckler estimates the risk before participating. Being ejected or arrested for that kind of disruption is often the desired outcome to add impact and importance to the protest.

What is defined as good or evil is often ascribed to a deity — or rather what the deity told the prophet or confidant. The Judeo-Christian Bible tells us that God himself spoke the Ten Commandments from Mount Sinai and wrote them with his own finger on tablets of stone (Exodus 20:1; 31:18).

The belief goes on to claim that God gave the Ten Commandments to Moses, who used them as the basis of the world's most popular religions. They formed the core definitions of good and evil. But prior to that, there were still both laws and recognised community standards relating to good and evil, by which people could assess their actions. They had been evolved by a filtration process of common actions that benefited or harmed the wellbeing of the community. And they have always come from MA.

CHAPTER 7

War and Peace

Only the dead have seen the end of war.
Plato

This time I've borrowed from Tolstoy, but again I'm only using his title, because for my purposes the content of the giant novel simply boils down to the obvious: that war and peace exist as natural and expected states of the human condition. What the novel doesn't go into is the 'why' of war and peace. Rather it is about armies and their supporters engaged before battle, during battle and after battle.

MA has determined that we are warlike creatures. We prefer to put more resources into fighting each other than the common enemies of mankind. It seems easy enough to suspend war in the obvious belief that peace is more beneficial. Here we have a clash between what we say and what we do.

Every public panel discussion puts forward the need for good moral behaviour and audience members smile and nod their heads. There should be no wars and only peace. Comments follow about how everybody should do the right thing. The acid test is around the word 'should'. When a machine fails, somebody will tell us that it 'should' work. Somehow, 'should' gets us off the hook, as though by uttering the word the fault is fixed. But telling us that our car should go when it is has broken down doesn't start the engine for us to make the journey. It simply allows the commentator to minimise responsibility for the problem.

While we may see war as yet another matter we have to deal with and, if we accept MA, it looks like a component. Certainly, it is part of the MA mix but it is not an independent component like, say, laws or comparisons — both of which we've talked about. War is actually a consequence of several components of MA. It is seen as a solution when other demands of MA are not met. War could be seen as the enforcer of some MA components.

Let's look at what we mean by war. In fundamental terms war takes place when two opposing ideologies cannot co-exist through tolerance or negotiation — although

CHAPTER 7 War and Peace

bear in mind that negotiation is a kind of war in itself. Country A wants to control country B (which doesn't want to be controlled) and so declares war on it. Country B retaliates in defence. Both countries raise armies and press their civilians into supporting those armies. The war ends when one country accepts that it cannot win and allows the victorious country to rule it. Of course, there are many variations on the classical war. Third-party countries may join in because they have alliances to honour. Other countries (for example Switzerland in the Second World War) may not want to be involved and so declare neutrality. Small-stake wars can go on without resolution for a hundred years. Whatever the cause of the war, the fundamental driver remains the same: a conflict over viewpoints.

Although conflict seldom leads to wars on a country versus country basis, skirmishes aside, it is continuous and abundant at a lower level in our everyday lives. Each of us has mini wars going on all the time. Whenever we don't get our own way, a conflict comes into existence. We may (as in the style of a traditional war) decide not to contest it — which amounts to surrender. Let's say our next-door neighbour has built a solid brick boundary wall encroaching five centimetres into our property, thus technically taking some of our land. We ask him to move the wall to where it should be. He tells us to get lost because he's paid a lot of money for the wall and, anyway, you can't even see the difference the five centimetres has made. Do we make an issue of it, maybe going to court, where, between us, we will spend more money on legal fees than the wall cost? Or do we shrug our shoulders and say leave it where it is and invite our neighbour in for a barbecue? We have a choice between war and peace, both at some cost. Apart from the material cost, we have our self-esteem to consider. Maybe our acquiescence is seen as a sign of weakness. Okay, we can't notice the five centimetres and it doesn't affect our lifestyle, but why should the neighbour be allowed to get away with it?

We've all seen the lengths to which neighbours will go over what look like minor points of disagreement. They make entertaining reading in the social media. Most observers privately enjoy witnessing the struggle and are thankful they are not the protagonists. Many also enjoy giving an opinion on what they would have done and what should now happen.

Every time we get out of bed in the morning, we enter a multi-conflict zone. Many of the conflicts are so small that they hardly register. A sock is missing from our drawer, our breakfast eggs are a little overdone, the traffic on our trip to work is unyielding, our desk at work doesn't have as nice a view as the one next to us, our superior is not treating us with the respect we deserve, we should have been promoted before that other fellow. So it goes all day. Although we may quite like our job, we believe we would be much happier without any conflicts or obstacles. The truth is, that would never be a possibility because the components of MA make conflict essential. Hence it is not a separate component of MA but a consequence of several components.

Conflict, on its multiplicity of levels, is unavoidable. More than that, it is a driving force in our lives. It is often via conflict that we advance. Nobody wins and nobody loses conflicts all of the time. Those who win more than they lose, subject to how high the conflict stakes are, get more goodies in life. Because money is power in reserve, those who win money conflicts are more highly rewarded than those who win fights behind the pub on Saturday night.

Conflict is also subject to sublimation. Instead of going to war with France, we send our football team there to stage a contained, symbolic war in a stadium. Once that war is over, we accept the outcome — which can give a high degree of satisfaction to the victorious country and equivalent disappointment to the loser. Occasionally, the conflict on the football field is not satisfying enough, and opposing supporters will take it to the next level of physically fighting with each other.

All competitive sport is war by another name. While I may play tennis for the exercise and the fresh air and sunshine that comes from being outdoors, I want to win for the same reason that, if I had a gun in my hand in a war, I would want to kill somebody from an opposing army. The stakes at tennis are obviously not as high as those in an armed battle, but they serve the same purpose of advancing my cause via conflict.

And we shouldn't confine ourselves to sport to see war-sublimation at work. Any situation where there are opposing views or the desire for opposing outcomes qualifies for a sublimated war. I have a friend who wants to make sure he gets first choice of the overhead locker space in an aircraft when he travels. He positions himself at the front of the boarding queue and scurries down the air bridge at a speed that nobody will pass him. Few people see this minor conflict the way he does, so he usually wins by getting his way. I wonder what would happen if he came upon a speedier opponent. It could get ugly.

No matter what we are doing, we're competing, whether we see it that way or not. Many gentle folks don't like the thought of winners and losers, or that they should cause somebody else to feel defeated and degraded. But that's all it is: a thought. MA forces them into action, disguised as reluctance or not.

When my father died at ninety-two, having lived a very active and competitive life, my brother and I put a notice in the paper, which said 'peace at last'. When I think about it, that made the assumption that Dad had been looking forward to unworried idleness. But nothing could be further from the truth. He loved conflict. He wanted to win at bowls, to be smarter than the next person when it came to investing, to have a better view of Port Phillip Bay than other people, to go the fruit market on Saturday morning and bargain the price down on a bunch of bananas. He didn't want peace. In fact, very few people who die look forward to resting in total peace, despite the popularity of RIP plaques. In earthly terms, eternal peace is boring.

Lions are not peaceful creatures and neither are we. We could argue that we are the most conflicted creatures on Earth. Lions kill to eat and survive, but we kill (or at least have to win) for a whole lot of additional reasons, most of them cerebral. MA has served us up so many reasons for conflict that we could never count them. Going back to the chapter pointing out how many laws, rules and regulations we live under, they are only part of the indicators for conflict. For example, take the broad, and now popular term 'harassment'. Practically any interaction with another person can be labelled harassment, simply because it is the eye of the beholder, and that position is currently strengthening. As soon as the harassee declares harassment, conflict is automatically born with the harasser. It may be resolved by an explanation or an apology, or it may end up in court, but there will be a conflict, a victor and a vanquished.

On a broader front, the media continually brings us news of violent conflicts around the world and, in our more mellow moments, we ask ourselves, why can't people live in peace? There is so much need and so much misery in the world that could be eradicated if we simply disengaged from wars and redirected the expenditure toward humanitarian causes. But while practically everybody would agree with that in principle, it will never be achieved, simply because our MA forces wars upon us. If we had the power to stop every current war today there would be a replacement lot almost immediately. While our MA remains the way it is, wars and the whole gradation of lesser disputes will continue. In other words, we're stuck with conflict in its many guises.

Wars, it should be noted, are not only about one group taking the possessions of another. Some of the most shocking losses of life through warlike aggression have been inflicted over philosophical or religious beliefs — or simply ways of living. Many of them are based on the fear that an emerging group of people will grow in strength to the point where they become dominant. Therefore, they must be eradicated before that can happen. Both the seizing of possessions and the fear of future domination can combine. And although history has shown us this kind of behaviour repeating right up until the present day, and we publicly deplore the destruction, we are powerless to learn from it or prevent it happening in the future. The reason? Our MA drives us to it, and while the solution available is suspension, we choose conflict. So many people have said the Holocaust will never be allowed to happen again — and it probably won't, certainly involving the Third Reich and six million Jews, but similar atrocities have happened since. Joseph Stalin is credited with ordering the killing of around twenty million people. Today we are witnessing appalling treatment of Uyghur Muslims by the Chinese government while the Shi'ite-Sunni conflict is the most deadly and unsolvable conflict in the Middle East, and it is between Muslims — supposedly sharing a common religion. Throughout recorded history wars over possessions, beliefs and fear have continued, and there is no sign of them abating. Quite the contrary, because technology is handing us more efficient ways to control and kill one another.

Changing our MA is a tantalising proposition. Maybe a future human will be created with a modified MA. But who or what would do the creating? We might eventually see the error of our Mind Architecture and want to place into the universe a better version of us. And if we are clever enough with the technology required, we might eradicate, or at least reduce, conflict. But for us now, and looking into the foreseeable future, we have to just suck it up. Better we understand it and work with it than wish or pretend it were different.

CHAPTER 8

Life and Death

All investigations of Time, however sophisticated or abstract, have at their true base the human fear of mortality.
Thomas Pynchon

MA gives us a unique double-sided view of mortality. There is no other living creature on Earth that has our level of understanding of life and death.

It is a universal MA principal that every life form will try to preserve its own life. Every living thing resists death. If that were not the case, life would cease very quickly on Earth and then we'd be faced with the interesting question of why it existed in the first place.

Human MA shares the same life-preservation component as other living creatures. In addition to the mental resolve we all share to keep living (with exceptions, such as suicide or the terminally ill requesting euthanasia), our bodies automatically fight against dying. Deprived of enough life supporting essentials like food, water or air, our bodies will make operational changes without our conscious approval so that we can survive longer than we would under 'normal' operation.

In addition to what we may call the will to live, our MA provides us with the comprehension of death. This is something of a conundrum. If we know we are going to die, why do we resist it until our last breath? One reason is fear of the unknown. We have made up many variants of supernatural explanations of what happens to our awareness after we die. Unlike the certainty that we will die, we don't know what happens, if anything, after the event. Another reason is that we value awareness and all that goes with it. We want to prolong it as long as possible.

Most religions offer a 'life after death' outcome to affiliates without one shred of scientific supporting evidence. In some cultures, ghosts are considered factual, along with unseeable spirits, while in others death is offered as a better alternative to life. In the meantime, the living are continually looking for signs that there is a supernatural world waiting for them through death's doorway.

CHAPTER 8 Life and Death

My mother died of cancer when she was sixty-two. During one painful session of radiotherapy (chemotherapy had not yet been perfected) she recalled that she had the sensation of somebody massaging her feet, and when she looked down to the end of the bed, there was her long-dead aunty. My mother told me how Aunty had led her away to meet a number of deceased relatives, including my much-loved grandmother. They told my mother that it was not yet time to join them and that she must go back and continue her life for a short while longer. They would be waiting for her. Since my mother was neither religious nor a believer in the supernatural, I saw her experience as either real or the effect of a pain-killing drug that had produced an illusion that she wanted to have. In any case, it gave her an easier path to death.

There is a popular belief that the death state is so much better than the life state that if we knew all about it while alive, we'd be topping ourselves to make the change. While I'd like to think that death is better than life, I have no way of knowing. Although stories like my mother's make attractive contemplation, I must accept that I'll have to wait until I die to find out for myself.

The late Stephen Hawking, one of the greatest thinkers ever, was convinced that there was no god and no afterlife.

'There is no god,' he wrote. 'No one directs the universe. For centuries, it was believed that disabled people like me were living under a curse that was inflicted by God. I prefer to think that everything can be explained another way, by the laws of nature.

We are each free to believe what we want and it's my view that the simplest explanation is that there is no god. No one created the universe, and no one directs our fate. This leads me to a profound realisation: there is probably no heaven and afterlife either. There is no reliable evidence for it, and it flies in the face of everything we know in science. I think that when we die, we return to dust. But there is a sense in which we live on, in our influence, and in the genes we pass to our children.'

As various members of my family have died, most of them have earned the send-off wish to 'rest in peace' or 'peace at last'. Because dead bodies do not move, we interpret this as being peaceful and therefore something that the dead person probably likes. As in the case of my father, peace is unlikely to be what most people want when they die. Certainly, death offers freedom from pain, and debt, and from every other kind of life struggle that we are not enjoying, but it also deprives the deceased from physical exhilaration, or the happiness that comes from achievement. Nobody that I know, who has died, wanted to rest in peace. They may not have been happy with some aspects of their lives, but they didn't look forward to doing nothing and going nowhere. Our parting wish should be more along the lines of Jack Kevorkian, famous death doctor, who used to whisper to his euthanasia patients, right at the end: 'have a good journey'.

Part of MA is to invent that which we cannot prove scientifically with fact. While scientific investigation has destroyed a lot of the man-made mumbo-jumbo about many subjects, what happens to awareness after death remains a mystery. Various people, such as my mother, have claimed to have experienced what lies on the other side of death and a few prophets have passed on what they claim a deity told them about the death state, but it requires faith without scientific proof to accept it. Faith is one of those emotive words that polite people don't like to question because it threatens to introduce disbelief into somebody's intimate and personal relationship with something they hold dear. Destroying faith is almost indecent and certainly not polite. I don't want to win an argument with somebody over faith, which is why I avoid debating the subject.

CHAPTER 9

Love

Love isn't something you find.
Love is something that finds you.
Loretta Young

As I've watched David Attenborough's inspiring television nature documentaries on how animals live, I've often wondered if they fall in love, as we experience it, or are they simply carrying out that part of their MA which obliges them to mate to continue the species. Fish mate without touching each other. The female simply leaves her eggs for the male to fertilise. One look at them does the orgasmic trick. Flowers entice bees to do the fetching and carrying for them to mate. We can assume that love does not play a role for fish, flowers or bees. Moving up the intelligence chain we might change our view a little when it comes to elephants, baboons or dolphins — although the imperative of species survival has a lot to do with propelling them to carry out what their MA has forced upon them.

Our human MA has made mating so complex it is a wonder that we can reproduce at all. Our penis and vagina fundamental activities are overridden, not just by in-fashion physical techniques, but also by ever changing, persistent analyses and debates which never allow us to settle on a standardised mating procedure. We get sidetracked by sexual preferences, by bodily dimensions, by what's cool and what isn't, by what's sexually offensive and what's acceptable, by the laws and mores governing what's implied by a facial expression or a style of dressing. We can list all of these under the heading 'display'. Display has now become more important than sexual intercourse. However, having said that, the world has still managed to overpopulate.

Then there's love, an emotion that can lead to a sexual outcome, but more than often doesn't. The vast majority of books and songs are written about love, either directly or indirectly. In its simplest form, a man and a woman meet, love is created and they mate. But there are so many familiar variants on this that the mating outcome becomes minor. A man and a man meet (or a woman and a woman), love is created and they simulate mating but it does not fit the definition too well. A man and a woman meet, love is created but they may not mate for a variety of reasons, the most common of which is that they are married to somebody else. We buy a puppy; love is created but we don't mate. We go to a football match; love is created for our team, but neither players nor spectators are there to mate. And so it goes on. Love is created in all kinds of situations which do not lead to mating, just as mating can occur where there is no love. Few men love the sex worker they've just mated with, nor does the sex worker love them.

Bear in mind that we're not talking about the even broader definition of love such as the love of money, or the love of a classic car or a spectacular sunset. I'm talking about the love that is created when we interact with living creatures. In this sense, while the love can be intense and romantic, its statistical destination is only occasionally mating.

It has taken all the above arguments to bring us to the point that what we generally categorise as love is an emotion that can arise from a huge variety of experiences. And, you've guessed it: love is part of MA, and at its most highly developed form in humans.

While it may be convenient to combine 'falling in love' with simply 'loving', the two are not made of the same stuff, even though we use the word loosely as a cover-all. The love we feel for our puppy has different components to the love we feel for a man or a woman. They are what we might call twin components of MA but they are not identical.

First, let's consider that intense, out-of-control emotion we feel for another person. It has been likened to a sickness. We'll call it romantic love. Some people experience this only once (or in some cases, never) in their lives while others fall in romantic love many times. It seldom retains its intensity for long. Now, take a deep breath.

Romantic love is a virus.

Because it cannot be observed wriggling around under a microscope doesn't mean it is not a virus. It is a psychological virus and acts the same way as a physical virus. We catch it from interacting with somebody else, there is no cure for it, and it decides when it will leave us. There are long-term and short-term romantic love viruses. Many remain after the cause of the infection has departed. Unrequited love is one of these. Others leave the afflicted one quickly, such as when we say goodbye to the date that didn't work out, in spite of heart-flutters when we first met.

A journalist friend of mine used to go to the jewellery

trade fair in Hong Kong every year. It was great fun, meeting up with other journalists from all over the world who had been invited to see and write about Hong Kong in its bid to become a leading jewellery innovation centre. Its jewellery fair generated plenty of positive publicity, largely because the journalists were treated so royally. Angus, we'll call him, became especially friendly with writers and editors from England and America, mostly young women, whose talents usually matched their good looks.

Angus met Jenny at one of the many lavish functions put on by the Hong Kong jewellery show organisers. She was from New York, petite, pretty, articulate and an admirable writer. Fleeting affairs were common at events like these. They seldom amounted to anything more than a fling that was forgotten after the week was over and the journalists had gone home to resume their busy lives. What happened at the fair stayed at the fair. But on this occasion Angus became badly infected by the romantic love virus. He returned to Australia unable to concentrate on anything without thinking about Jenny. They exchanged furtive letters and telephone calls. They were both married to good, blameless partners from whom they had to keep their mutual yearning. They admitted to each other that their dearest wish was that the attraction would leave them in peace — but that only fed the flames. The next opportunity to meet would be at the fair the following year. It was torture, but they decided that when they met again, they would try to work out a way to spend their lives together. The months dragged by. Finally, February came around, along with Angus's invitation to attend the fair. One problem was that Jenny had changed jobs during the year and was no longer covering jewellery. She had to take a week of her holidays and tell her husband she had an assignment in Hong Kong.

Angus boarded his flight in Melbourne and settled into his seat daydreaming about Jenny. Soon they would be together. The flying hours moved painfully by until they were on final approach to Hong Kong's Kai Tak airport. Angus suddenly felt a cold wave go through him. The love virus had departed. Even as the plane landed Angus dreaded seeing Jenny. Did she now feel the same about him? Did love viruses meet secretly for consultations? He thought so, because when they met in the hotel foyer it was awkward. Although she didn't admit it, he suspected that the virus had left her too. They went back to being just acquaintances cast into acting like lovers. She only stayed two nights and they slept separately. He silently cheered as her taxi left for the airport. They never communicated again.

If ever there was a demonstration of romantic love being a virus, my friend Angus experienced it. Of course, you could explain it away as 'coming to his senses', or being overcome with guilt for how he'd felt and acted, but in my experience these factors are seldom strong enough to cure a powerful love virus. Angus told me he bitterly regretted what he'd done. While any of us may resist acting on the romantic love virus when it threatens to make us behave contrary to community standards, and be praised for our moral fortitude, that does not make the virus go away; it just means that we suffer in silence for as long as it takes to leave us.

Although increasing age makes the romantic love virus more impractical to act upon, nobody is immune to its exhilaration and pain, no matter how old they are. Elderly men suffer from an unreciprocated romantic love virus attack over younger women, and society dismisses them as silly old buggers. Mostly, unless they are very rich and powerful, they just put up with the pain until it leaves them or, in some cases, they die dreaming of the lovemaking that could have been — were they only younger and circumstances different. The romantic love virus is celebrated and encouraged among the young, but is not welcome in the elderly. The best they can hope for is to be attacked by a less virulent form of the virus, which will eventually leave them alone.

We can look upon the romantic love virus as good or bad, as vital or trivial, as powerful or weak, but make no mistake, it is unavoidable and always lurking in the shadows. It is part of MA.

Now let's look at the other kind of love. It is powerful too, but more like a long-distance runner than a sprinter. Boy meets girl when they are in their early twenties. They are both hit with the romantic love virus. They live together for a while, then marry — largely because they want children, and marriage is a better environment for family-making. Over time, the romantic love virus leaves them and they look at the form of love they now have. They respect and tolerate each other's needs and points of view, even though they may differ in many ways; they enjoy each other's company; they are ready to compromise; they care about each other's wellbeing and try to protect it; they fulfil the sexual needs of one another. They are in love, and you would say this is an enviable marriage. But their love is not romantic love because that virus has departed — probably before they were even married. What they have is a highly successful arrangement. Yes, there is physical affection there, but it is the same kind of affection that exists between many people or living creatures that will never be temporarily obsessed with one another. They are responding to an arrangement that suits both parties — often for different reasons.

Sexual desire can be quite separate from love. The

fairy-tale romance is that love and sexual desire run in parallel. When the ideal couple meet, they totally fulfil both requirements for each other. This is the expectation that many religions and ethical authorities espouse. It is what nice people want for themselves and the rest of the world. It is a form of purity. It is an 'ought'. But the truth is that love and sexual desire seldom run in parallel, especially over a protracted time period. On the whole, men and women make do with what they get, fearing, perhaps, that they cannot get any closer to their ideal. Many fill the gaps with other outlets like affairs, pornography or prostitution.

We might be forgiven for blaming MA for failing to invariably bind love with sexual desire. It doesn't seem to bother a rooster as he chases a hen he fancies around the fowl yard. Animals seem to have it better organised than we do. Love, if it exists among animals, doesn't get in the way of reproduction.

CHAPTER 10

Artistry

Those who do not want to imitate anything, produce nothing.
Salvador Dali

Being a music lover and passable pianist, I fed the question of music into my channel in relation to MA. The answer that came back was a rebuke. I'd been too narrow. Music was only one form of artistic expression. Nevertheless, let's deal with music first.

Although music is usually delivered via sound, it doesn't have to be. I am not a professional musician, but I can read a score and know roughly what the music will sound like. Of course, if I'd never heard music before or if the score was for an unfamiliar solo instrument, I'd be lost. Likewise, I can sit with my eyes closed and hear a symphony in my head. Thus, music relies partly on what we can physically hear matched up with what we can remember.

Let's talk about the more familiar forms of music, produced and received via sound waves that travel through the air. Here, direct transmission takes over and memory plays a minor role. Some performed music is purely for communication or ceremony, like the playing of the last post at military events. Warning chimes when your car door is left open, or when the lift has arrived at your floor, or the annoying music played over the telephone system while you're holding on; none of these is intended to induce singing, dancing or even affection. They are no more than signals that have employed music to take the place of voices and words, and reassure that the connection is maintained. Sound effects fall into the same category. The aim of all these is simply to communicate a practical message.

So, down to real music, sung or played. Do humans have it on their own? The jury is out on that one. Whales, dolphins and birds appear to sing to one another, but how much is communication and how much is artistic expression? Humans have certainly adopted music as an emotional or sometimes technical outpouring. I can be moved to tears by some classical music. Others will emotionally respond to a love song or a rock band. They are all part of the same thing, divided only by personal taste and, although not everybody would say they like music, they cannot escape it, either internally or externally. And yes, music is part of MA. There is no race on Earth that does not have some form of music, some religious and some secular.

However, while every collective expresses itself in music, not every individual within that collective likes it or wants to participate in it. Music is not all-inclusive. Everybody has a choice.

Having said that, it is worth acknowledging the role that music plays in movies, most genres of television and, more recently, accompanying computer-based games. Music is so deeply ingrained in entertainment and media that we hardly notice its presence yet, judging by its continual and universal usage, it has become essential. Background music for visuals (as distinct from purely musical performance) tells the viewer how to interpret what he or she is seeing. Let's say we create a scene in which the camera pans slowly across an old house. By adding different types of music, we can make that house tragic, sad, comical, stately, trivial or holy when we look at it. Music is a message from the director and it suggests how we should interpret what we are being shown — and we virtually always accept it.

Music is but one form of artistic expression — which is where MA comes into it. People have been arguing about the definition of art for centuries. My channel came up with this: Art is the reinterpretation into a form different from the original. Love becomes a song. A sunset becomes a painting. A life becomes a novel. A story becomes a ballet. It is the change of medium and its reinterpretation that produces the work of art.

It is probable that only human MA has that component of artistic expression and it manifests itself in the lives of every person, to a greater or lesser degree. Most artistic expression passes unnoticed. Unless the artist draws attention to the exhibition or performance of his or her work, artistic expression becomes background in everyday life.

The reason or the need for artistic expression is an intriguing subject and I'm tempted to submit it to my channel, but I'd be moving away from the purpose of this book. I'm dealing with what we are rather than why. But rest assured that artistic expression is a component of MA, very important to some people and less so to others.

CHAPTER 11

Time

*Time is free, but it's priceless. You can't own it,
but you can use it. You can't keep it,
but you can spend it.
Once you've lost it you can never get it back.*
Harvey Mackay

Like size, the starting point in the measurement of time is our own body. A human lifetime is somewhere between zero and 120 years. In cosmic terms, that is almost immeasurably brief. Yet we can have a sense of there being 'plenty of time'. Our attitude to time comes from MA. An entity whose life span is two billion years sees time no differently to a particle that lives for a fraction of a millisecond when it is based upon comparison with similar entities around it. In isolation, there is no conception of time. It becomes both infinite and infinitesimal together.

Time, therefore, is simultaneously a perception and a fixed measure. Our perception of personal time varies enormously. During certain activities time seems to pass quickly whereas under different circumstances it seems to drag. Yet, if we continually referred to a clock, we would see that time clicks along in equal measures. The question is, which is right, our perception or the clock? The answer is: both. And just to confuse the subject further, Einstein's physics tells us, and it has been proven by experiment, that time slows the faster we move. At the speed of light, it stops altogether. Nearing the speed of light, we would appear to ourselves, as we looked in a mirror, to be aging 'normally' whereas everybody else not up to our speed would be aging more rapidly. There have been many science fiction movies devoted to exploring the anomalies of time because we are both ruled and fascinated by it.

In MA terms, time is how we perceive it, running parallel with its various scientific and mechanical definitions. It follows that my perceived time is not the same as your perceived time, and even my own perceived time varies according to my personal activities. I may take you to a concert, which I enjoy so much that it passes all too quickly, whereas you may sit there bored and find that

CHAPTER 11 Time

time drags intolerably. Our clock tells us that we've spent the same amount of time at the concert but have perceived that time differently.

Along with the wide variation in perception, MA provides us with a means of consensus relating to time so that we can interact with one another. Sol, our man in the cave, doesn't have much use for a clock. He would have noticed the lengthening and shortening of seasonal sunlight and the changes in other external markers of time, and he may have felt his own pulse and become aware that it could be used as a measure. But he'd be much more aware of his personally perceived time which varied according to what he was doing. A clock would have been pointless because he was not trying to coordinate with anybody else. It is only when numbers of people interact that external, purely mechanical devices become necessary. MA has provided us with a dual outlook on time but it is far from perfect. Perception and reality never match up very well and time is no exception.

MA bestows upon us two first cousins of time: anticipating and remembering. Do other life forms anticipate, or plan ahead, or have goals? Do they lie down and remember past events with either joy or remorse? The answer depends upon whether we choose to separate survival instinct from thoughts that are not survival driven. In the middle of summer, does a bear know and think about hibernating during winter? Does a male salmon know that ahead of him is a fight against strong currents and other obstacles before he can spawn? There is no doubt that many animals remember, but we cannot tell whether that process is part of their survival MA or, as in our case, an optional ability provided by our MA, with both entertainment and practical applications.

As far as conscious planning and anticipation are concerned, there is no doubt that these are part of MA — and are shared to a certain extent with other living creatures. If we've ever watched a pride of lions working as a team to trap a four-legged meal, we'll acknowledge planning and anticipation at work. When it comes to human MA, our plans can range over a much longer period and can be far more complex.

MA also confers upon us a sense of, and need for, history. Again, comparing this with other living creatures, we seem to be unique. While history accumulates instinctive wisdom in animals, it does not seem to play an ongoing, contemplative role in their lives. We may well ask, why is history so important to us?

It has to do with our view of time. If we acknowledge past, present and future, then we must populate the past with events to give it dimension. Thinking about past years, we naturally draw comparisons with the present and look for patterns that may affect the future. In chapter five we discussed judging our worth by comparison with other people. The contemplation of history is similar, in that it enables us to compare how things used to be with how they are now and how they might be in the future.

The truth of the old saying 'history repeats itself' depends upon how you define 'repeats'. Stock market speculators have spent decades trying to find enough past common patterns to accurately predict future price movements. While they can certainly identify general trends that repeat, it is changes in timing that sometimes makes, but more often, breaks them. The same goes for most predictive practices. While they may be accurate in principle, they rely on timing to succeed.

The reasons why history broadly repeats itself is because human behaviour is dictated by MA which, in principle, has not changed over millennia. The interplay of its components will always have repeating outcomes, such as wars, economic upturns and downturns, anarchy and suppression, addiction and indifference, but the severity and timing of those outcomes is never the same because there are changing weightings of MA's components. The component of change in MA is very powerful. That's why this book doesn't promise absolutes or cures. Understanding MA is a tool, not a solution.

CHAPTER 12

Change

We live in a moment of history where change is so speeded up that we begin to see the present only when it is already disappearing.
R. D. Laing

Change is the most overworked subject at seminars. The underlying reason is that a seminar, almost by definition, is a meeting to discuss and disseminate change. The attendees lap up change. What is the latest model, the new order, the incoming system that will replace the old one? How will things be different? Those who know first about change have a clear advantage.

Speakers continually remind us that the only constant is that things will change — as if we need to be told. In times of reminiscence, when we remember our childhood, we can often be quite shocked when we compare how life was then to how life is now. Looking in the opposite direction, when we listen to futurists, the magnitude of upcoming change is often difficult to grasp or accept. Mostly, it is frightening.

To reminisce about my own early childhood in Melbourne: I remember bread arriving by horse and cart, the heroic iceman delivering a huge block for our ice chest, groceries such as sugar and flour being taken from a bin, weighed, and placed in a paper bag while my mother chatted to the grocer and went over her long shopping list. To me, and to many older people, it seems like a life lived by somebody else.

We can also measure change by how fast mankind is accumulating knowledge. To quote David Russell Schilling:

> Buckminster Fuller created the "Knowledge Doubling Curve". He noticed that until 1900 human knowledge had doubled approximately every century. By the end of World War II knowledge was doubling every 25 years. Today things are not as simple, because different types of knowledge are attributed to having different rates of growth. For example, nanotechnology knowledge is doubling

every two years and clinical knowledge every 18 months. But, on average, human knowledge is doubling every 13 months. According to IBM, the build out of the "internet of things" will lead to the doubling of knowledge every 12 hours.

Since that quote came from 2013, the numbers today would be even more startling. Knowledge probably now doubles every few minutes. There is a direct correlation between knowledge and change. Without increasing knowledge, change would slow down dramatically or might stall altogether.

The question then arises, why do we need change? 'Stop the World, I Want to Get Off!' was a 1961 musical whose title resonated with many people. It probably has even more sympathisers today. The rate of change is especially daunting for older people who have a longer timeline and steepening change curve to deal with. Many of them would like change to pause for a while so they can relax, understand, and catch up at their own pace. But they have no choice, just as there is no choice — apart from conscious suspension — in anything that is part of MA. While change is at its most potent in young adults, people of all ages make their contribution to it. Some of the most brilliant minds reside in old heads and some of the dullest people are young adults.

Change can be roughly divided into three categories, although one can turn into another over time. At the personal level there is micro-minutia change. Much of that is unconscious and automatic. Every physical action brings about change. When we breathe, when our heart pumps, when we blink — it all brings about change to the way things were a microsecond before. Much of that type of change is to do with how our bodies work and not attributable to the behavioural dictates of MA we're considering here.

Conversely, conscious personal change is very much imposed by MA. All our conscious endeavours have the intention to bring about change — although only a percentage of them succeed. We are forever trying to create more favourable conditions and outcomes in our lives. Some of it is expected and some merely hopeful. We'd like everything around us to give a better result than it does now. That might apply to the government, money, personal relationships, health, workplace, sports, our garden — in other words, everything we are involved in.

The push for personal change goes on all the time. It is a natural element of being human, and it probably applies to most other life forms too. In some ways it is a counterweight to death. If we are always working towards change for the better, maybe we can skirt around death, or at least delay its arrival.

CHAPTER 12 Change

Change that emanates from within us is either automatic or entirely private.

For that reason, we don't often see it as change, but just the normal way we go about living. To most of us, change is what's going on in the external world. It is the lifeblood of the media. Change makes news. We thrive on it. We'd feel cheated if our news source told us stories that didn't deal with or suggest change. When the media gets worried that there isn't enough change to provide content, it will poke a bear or two in the hope of starting some action that will lead to change. It might ask a champion when he intends to retire from playing tennis, or the Australian Prime Minister if there is leadership plot going on. While the media provides history and information about status quo matters, it is change that makes headlines and money.

Conscious change breaks down into four sequential elements. The first is imagination: the idea that comes into somebody's head of how something ought to be — but presently is not. The second is a plan to move from aspiration to realisation. The third is the execution of that plan. The fourth is completion of the change so that it becomes a part of life's public or private assets, or backdrop. It will not be permanent. It may be totally disregarded in the future, or modified through the same process that gave it birth. The sword that fought for and won change is the same sword that can kill it in favour of a new order.

From an MA perspective, change outside ourselves is more obvious. It is what we spend most time arguing over in private and public forums. This type of change can be consensual or dictatorial in nature. In other words, it can rise up as a consensus idea from the masses (the perceived prevention of global warming, for example) or it can be handed down from a single person with a convincing idea (Adolf Hitler, for example). In our personal lives we deal with change in how we dress, what we eat, who we befriend, how we make a living. Publicly, we see change discussed, sometimes furiously, in politics, big business and all kinds of group causes. How often we hear: 'things have to change!' We've become so used to the call for change that we expect to hear it brought into almost every discussion.

We can torment ourselves by asking whether change is really for the good. Are we heading towards a better world? Were our parents and their parents happier than we are now? That brings up how we define happiness, and there are so many opinions here that we'd never get through them because happiness is measured empirically and is totally personal. The reality is that we must change. That often means going along with change that comes from outside. I don't design cars, but when the new model comes out, I generally accept the change it represents and embrace it. We assume that change is for the better, although that often turns out to be an illusion.

Looking ahead we ask ourselves if tomorrow is part of a great journey to Utopia. We'd probably be more comfortable with change if that were the known case. If we had a roadmap into the future that would show us where we are today and what lies at the end, we'd embrace change more readily. But most of us feel change is thrust upon us. Our feeling is correct. Change is part of MA and unavoidable. And so is its acceleration. Whoever or whatever built MA seems to want the human race to change ever more rapidly. I'm not putting forward the solution of a divine inventor, incidentally. We don't yet know enough about the cosmos to explain creation in general, let alone the creator of MA.

The question is whether change is synonymous with progress towards betterment or a pathway to ultimate destruction. Eventually, we'll find out. And because MA pressures us to change, there is the danger that we can succumb to that edict before looking at its benefits — or otherwise. We can all too easily overlook the danger of change for change's sake. In fact, we are now showing signs of doing just that. Everybody with an opinion or a cause, no matter how whacky, is advocating change towards their goal. In most Western countries it is currently obligatory to give them all a respectful hearing. But we must resist the temptation not to question change itself — simply because it is fuelled by MA. We should always ask whether it will increase our happiness or at least that of coming generations. Although a powerful component of MA, change should always have to pass the test of being beneficial to those affected by it.

Change is probably much bigger and far reaching than we acknowledge. After the Big Bang gave birth to the universe, science observed that the expansion of the universe was slowing down, like debris as it moves further away from the centre of an explosion. One school of thought was that the universe would eventually stop expanding, become static for a while and then begin to contract, finally reversing the Big Bang to become a singularity again. It was nicknamed the Big Crunch. But more recent measurements have revealed that the universe is back in expansion mode, and that the expansion is accelerating. It is possible that everything within the universe is affected in a similar way, and is now expanding too, including our knowledge and change. Although our cosmological measurements concentrate on visible matter like galaxies, why wouldn't this expansion go right down the MA level? The increase in knowledge and the change it enables are likely to be part of a universal shift, which includes the behavioural processes that MA forces upon us. Admittedly, this is a questionable theory, but since it came from my channel, I seriously ponder it.

Before we leave the subject of change, (and change it for something else), I should acknowledge a corollary branch of MA that is attached to it. If we were not programmed to accept our rate of change, it wouldn't have brought us to where we are today. Our development would have been arrested when we were at a primitive stage, maybe single cells living in water. At best, we'd still be hunter/gatherers. And there is the possibility that another species, maybe from the anthropoid group whose MA contained the seeking and acceptance of greater change, might be ruling Earth and be now hounding us out from under logs and other habitats. Hopefully they would have cared for the environment better than we have.

Change is somewhat deceptive. Does change happen to us or do we create it? MA compels us to change, so we have no choice. We do create change, but it runs only at the speed we can tolerate. It always has. History reveals periods of pace variation in change. From such a position we can deduce that, if we imagine change as an infinite line, the speed we move along that line is regulated by our tolerance for change.

To better understand change, we can look at the way we treat food. There is a parallel. We must eat to maintain life, just as we must change to satisfy MA. But we can decide what we eat and how often we eat, just as we can decide what we change and how often we make those changes.

Just where change can lead us, and what determines it, is one of those questions for which we must content ourselves with no answer — for the time being, at least.

CHAPTER 13

Obstacles Create Happiness

*The greater the obstacle,
the more glory in overcoming it.*
Moliere

As my channel was revealing the workings of MA, I was reminded of one of its revelations from many years ago. At that stage I had not identified my channel for what it was, nor had I given it credit for good ideas.

The upshot of that early channelling episode resulted in me writing a book called *The Lore of Obstacles*. Although the manuscript found a small publisher, it never went ahead because my life took an unexpected turn and I didn't have the time to go through the process of bringing it to market. And there it may have died. But when I came to writing about Mind Architecture, *The Lore of Obstacles* suddenly became relevant again because I recognised it as one of the more important components of MA.

Let me begin with a pivotal assumption: The purpose of living is to experience happiness. This is the only way we can make sense out of bothering with an earth-bound existence. If life exists for any other reason than the pursuit of happiness, we don't have to put up with it. There are many ways to end our lives before natural causes inevitably dismantle us.

Happiness is counter-balanced by unhappiness. While there are many names we can give unhappiness there is only one reason for its existence: to identify happiness. Light can be recognised only when there is darkness as well.

Happiness can come from anything we experience. There are fundamental experiences like basic food and shelter. If we lack either, it will bring happiness to attain them. But once they are provided, they are quickly taken for granted — like air or gravity. It is what we build on top of those basic sufficiencies that defines happiness in affluent societies and therefore becomes the attraction to continue living.

As soon as we add taste and style to food, we are building happiness above fundamental sustenance. Currently, the world, and Australia in particular, is in the grip of a food craze. On one hand is the global scientific challenge of increasing food supply to sustain life whilst, on the other, programs like *MasterChef* emphasise the Western phenomenon of food doubling as entertainment.

Depending upon the wealth of the society in which it is measured, what is regarded as happiness in one can be a fundamental attainment in another.

The need for fundamentals is a simple live or die proposition, whereas happiness comes armed with unseen obstacles. If it were not, we would be simply moving from one happiness to the next and we know that there is no lasting satisfaction in endless, unpunctuated happiness. It quickly runs out of steam.

Happiness comes at a price. That price is overcoming obstacles. The obstacles come in many guises to fulfil their hugely variable, but essential role in enabling happiness to be created. They can be physical obstacles like stairways or heavy objects, financial barriers like needing a loan, or emotional challenges like anxiety. They are often dressed in a cloak of fear or loathing because they stand between us and the outcome we want. Yet when we overcome them and look back, we are grateful for them for having been there to overcome and trigger our happiness payoff.

Happiness is the feeling we get when we attain something we like or we want. It can be a new car, a job, sexual gratification, appreciation of something we've done, or simply witnessing something intangible like a musical performance.

A happiness event is seen as a whole from a distance, where the division between the objective and its path to attainment is barely detectable. But close up, they become separated. One is the end product, happiness, while the other is the overcoming of the obstacle that leads to it.

Obstacles and happiness form the pattern of life as we experience it. We live by knowing and often quoting contrasts which are the rails upon which we run. Good and evil; night and day; beautiful and ugly; they are all setting the parameters by which we live and judge our circumstances. Our marriage vows enshrine them: 'for richer, for poorer, in sickness and in health . . .' Thus, we can identify a fundamental driver of human nature, which is part of the MA mix.

What about winning the lottery, we may ask? Where's the obstacle? First, of course, is having to buy a ticket. Now imagine there is a knock on our front door. We open it and find a well-dressed man who tells us that we've won first prize in a lottery. Do we demand the cheque and then slam the door in his face? Of course not. Instead, the lore of obstacles begins to operate. Do we believe this man is genuine? Why wouldn't he have telephoned or emailed first? Is he going to barge into our house and rob or injure us? Even if he is genuine, he will require our ID, oblige us to fill in receipt and release forms and maybe attend a handing over ceremony at which we might be required to make a speech. Even after we have overcome the obstacles associated with actually securing the money, we have the obstacle of finding somewhere to store it, who to tell about our win, and what to spend it on. These may be seen as minor obstacles before the win, but they grow considerably in stature afterwards and we cannot move forward until we deal with them.

When we consider the ramifications of 'unearned wealth', like winning a lottery, quite a few obstacles emerge from the shadows. Ask anybody if they'd like to win twenty- million-dollars and they will almost certainly say yes. Some of them, of course, will give it all away and their happiness payoff will be the gratitude of the recipients. But if we question those who intend to spend it on themselves, we will usually find that they run out of ideas before they run out of money.

Few lottery winners benefit, long term, from the money they acquire. A study done in England on football pool winners showed that the vast majority of the winners quickly divested themselves of the money they had won. Many of them lost spouses, health and even the modest savings they had before their big win.

Inherited money has a similar effect. The relatives, waiting around the dying rich man's bedside, dream of the money he will leave them. In doing so, they are each visiting their obstacle collections and looking at the carnage they intend to carry out. Often, their lives will fall apart because the unearned money has, in fact, robbed them of their obstacles and therefore their happiness. Those least affected by a big win already have wealth and simply add the money to their total.

There is a warning here to those of us who want to help others. I have a friend who was well-off enough to buy each of his two children a house when they married. The children, of course, were grateful, thus providing happiness for their father. But his generosity had an outcome that none of the parties anticipated. One of the children, while acknowledging the gift, wished it had been more because she would have been able to buy a house in a desired suburb. Within three years both children had lost their houses either as collateral for failed business ventures or attempting to buy that better house they'd wanted before, or ordering renovations they couldn't afford. They then turned to their parents and indignantly demanded more money so they could have another go.

CHAPTER 13 Obstacles Create Happiness

What my friend had done was to unwittingly steal his children's obstacles. It would have worked much better if he'd given them each enough for a deposit on a house and set them on their own course of obstacles and happiness as they moved towards eventual home ownership. In stealing their obstacles, he'd stolen their dreams.

Another friend, Paul, developed dementia. I knew him at his peak, when he was one of the most intelligent men I had ever met. When he and his wife decided to move to a seaside suburb not far from where I lived, Paul and I arranged to go walking early every Wednesday morning. These were times I looked forward to because we exercised our minds on one another in lively conversation as we strode along the harbour foreshore or took the narrow path on the cliff edge that overlooked the ocean. When Paul began to feel continually miserable, he thought he was suffering depression and would snap out of it once some business worries were resolved. But instead, he was diagnosed with Parkinson's disease. He wouldn't develop tremors like most Parkinson's sufferers, he was told, but this type would attack his brain, and dementia would follow.

Our walks shortened and we had to skirt around busy road crossings or steep slopes. Paul's once sparkling conversation degenerated to a few mumbles into his chest and a growing unsteadiness as he walked with the aid of a stick. He had to say goodbye to driving his Mercedes, going to the golf club or even taking himself to daytime movies by bus. Apart from being driven around by his wife, Paul's only regular weekly outing was his walk with me.

One day we arrived back at his home after our walk. Paul drew the key to his front door from his pocket and tried to get it into the lock. I stood and watched while he scraped the end of the key around and around, trying to push it into the barrel to unlock the door. It took five minutes before the key penetrated and he was able to let himself in.

During his struggle I was tempted to take the key from him, but I realised that I would steal his obstacle and the following happiness that winning this small challenge would bring him. When the key finally went in, I was rewarded with his grin of satisfaction. While we look upon helping as noble, it can often do more harm than good to the person we are trying to help.

Every one of our actions is preceded by thought operating on two interconnected levels, almost as though we have two minds. Without maybe realising it, those who developed today's computers copied the dual level of the human mind. We work and play in the conscious (RAM mode) while it, in turn, draws on the hard disk, or subconscious. The mind is far more complicated and powerful than a computer and our hard disk, our subconscious, often sends information and commands to the conscious without being requested to do so.

The conscious mind deals with the immediate needs of living, by feeling, loving, hating, smelling, laughing, planning, arguing, eating. You are conscious of being on that level now as you read. Apart from reading, you are functioning in many other sub-divisions of the conscious. You are dealing with the signals of the world around you. If somebody calls your name, your attention to this text will not prevent you from responding.

Whilst the conscious is both quick and aware, it does not compare in size or power to the subconscious, which is not only our warehouse of knowledge and instinct, but makes decisions independent of the conscious that profoundly affect our lives and, in all probability, the time and manner of our death.

Although the subconscious certainly belongs to us, it is very difficult to access. Its outer casing is our MA and inside are the elements that go to make up our personality. Our name might be on the door, establishing our ownership, but getting inside takes special keys like psychoanalysis or certain drugs.

The subconscious does not necessarily work in harmony with the conscious. In fact, it often works against the conscious mind by making us fail or succeed when logic tells us to expect just the opposite. In some ways, our life is under the influence of an unreliable entity, which may inflict pain upon us. But there is something we can do to combat the perversity of the subconscious. If we understand how the obstacles/happiness system works, we can train our conscious mind to take over much of their creation.

Obstacles come from two sources. One source, which we can control, is the conscious mind. These are the obstacles we think about, plan and overcome in the full light of awareness. We might, for instance, decide to build a boat, so we buy plans, gather materials and go to work. Our obstacle is the building and our happiness is the completion, launching and sailing.

The subconscious is the second source of obstacles and, unfortunately, is not a good judge of obstacles and happiness payoffs, which means that we are often served up the unpleasant or the unexpected. An obvious example is sickness. We don't catch a cold, we seek one, through our subconscious. You may well ask who needs a cold or a stroke or AIDS? The answer is the people who get them do.

CHAPTER 13 Obstacles Create Happiness

This is not to say we should accuse everybody who gets sick, or runs into trouble, of seeking eventual happiness, even though they unwittingly do so. They must be forgiven on the grounds that they did not wilfully plan their misfortunes, nor did they even suspect that they had created them.

Some careers offer an extra happiness payoff because they are in the obstacle business. The most familiar is that of the police officer, where obstacles are in abundance. If we are to believe the cop shows on television, there are as many battles within the station walls as there is crime in the streets. Not only do the cops snipe at one another but city hall is always threatening that if they don't hurry up with an arrest the mayor will become an obstacle to their promotion. Worse still, and fairly common for the likes of Dirty Harry, is the threat of being dismissed from the force. Screenplay writers are traditionally faced with trying to show why nobody should want to be a cop. He is poorly paid, continually battered and shot by criminals, never at home for his daughter's birthday, seldom available when his wife wants to make love, always being insulted by his superiors and forced into a diet of killer fast-food. If he is fired from the police department the only benefit he appears to lose is his service pension — which is a poor counterweight to the abuse he suffers. Moreover, there is little evidence that those like Dirty Harry even like their jobs. Harry never laughs, seldom smiles, and always looks as though he would rather be somewhere else. Why, we may well ask, does he continue being a cop?

The reason is that Harry is a person who needs even more obstacles than most people. He is an obstacle junkie. Not only does his career oblige him to overcome endless obstacles in enforcing the law but he has the internal obstacles of the police department and his personal life as well. His potential for happiness is therefore enormous, making him a paradox. Although we never see him celebrating overcoming any of his towering stack of obstacles, we know that Harry is one of the most fulfilled characters on the screen. Without being aware of it, we all appreciate Harry's example in the fulfilment and we watch, fascinated, to see if we dare emulate some of it.

Police exist as part of a chain we all create to provide community obstacles. We make laws we know some of us will break, then we set up a police force to catch us, a judicial system to punish us and a detention system to jail us. Remember that we are doing this to ourselves for eventual happiness. No outside force is responsible for this world's laws, their enforcement and punishment. Each of the links in the chain of law creates an obstacle. We can overcome them either by avoiding confrontation or by breaking them and then winning a battle of wits in court. If we decide not to break a law, then another

CHAPTER 13 Obstacles Create Happiness

obstacle pops up: How can we get everything we want and remain totally law abiding?

The whole system of law and its enforcement is in place to serve the need for obstacles in both those who are subject to the law and those who enforce it. It doesn't stop at criminal law either. The lesser laws, rules and manners of social behaviour are so vast that nobody can obey all of them all of the time, resulting in bountiful obstacles for everybody.

If you think this is an exaggerated viewpoint, imagine Dirty Harry and his colleagues in the dingy police station with the stale green walls, having achieved what we are led to believe they want: peace and order in the community. Harry sits at his desk cleaning his gun for the fourth time that day. Around him, the familiar chaos of too many crimes and not enough resources to solve them has gone. The detectives and the officers in uniform have all finished their paperwork. They sit reading newspapers, eating pizzas or drinking coffee. The cells are empty and the doors hang open. Suddenly Harry jumps to his feet and, in frustration, fires his revolver into the ceiling. 'I want some crime,' he bellows, and a chorus of agreement follows.

A career in the taxation department offers some similarities to the police force although it doesn't attract the same dramatic interest. The obstacles it hands out can be greater than those of the police. Most businesspeople would prefer a policeman, rather than a tax inspector, to knock on their door. Tax payments are a continuing obstacle, with a continuing happiness payoff that goes largely unacknowledged.

Communities have imposed the taxation obstacle upon themselves since history was first recorded. We may point out, rightly, that the collection of taxes is necessary to provide public utilities, which the individual cannot provide for himself. But these are obstacles dressed up as necessities. There are many continuing obstacles of this type. Religious rules operate as satellites to criminal and civil law. Extreme versions of most religions leave little time for activities outside the prescribed rituals. Viewed from the obstacle/happiness perspective, all religions demand sacrifices of free will in return for the happiness of feeling observant or even ecstatic.

If we accept that obstacles are fundamental to living and the only way to obtain happiness is to overcome them, then the creation of obstacles is worth our serious consideration. We will find that if we don't set out to create obstacles in our conscious minds, and because they are essential, the subconscious will step in and create them for us. The problem here is that the subconscious can be heavy handed and perverse when it is called upon to create obstacles. It can deliver illness, depression, and all kinds of adversities. But if we keep our conscious busy creating obstacles, we can take more control of them so that they suit the direction in which we want our lives to go.

Retirement brings men, especially, face to face with the need to create conscious obstacles when they leave their workplace carrying their gold watch. There is great danger to life when retirement is seen as a passport to do nothing or, at best, be entertained by television or travel for amusement.

We have all heard of men who leave their job at sixty-five in good health and die a couple of years later. They have unwittingly allowed their subconscious to set obstacles for them, one of which is a health problem that kills them. Every retiree, if he or she wants a long and interesting life after their main career is over, should carry out an obstacle review well before they retire and write a reminder list for themselves.

However, there is no point in setting obstacles that are impossible to overcome. If I chose, as an obstacle, breaking the world one hundred metres sprint record it would be a waste of time. Yet there are probably fifty runners who might contemplate breaking that record which, for them, would constitute an obstacle with a possibility of overcoming it.

There are no more obvious obstacles than those associated with the acquisition of money. Money sits squarely in front of us, an obstacle of fluctuating difficulty in acquisition and leading to happiness — also measured on a fluctuating scale. To most of us, money is the mountain range of life. Its summit is virtually infinite, and along the way there are plateaus, gentle slopes and a few deep ravines.

Money is power in storage, ready to be applied when we choose. Even if we leave it in storage and never apply it, there are still happiness payoffs in the knowledge that the power is available. In many ways, this type of fantasy can be as rewarding as using up the power. Let us say we accumulate ten million dollars and we leave it sitting in the bank. While it remains in the bank, we have the option of buying whatever we like. We could buy a million-dollar car, a multi-million-dollar house, or a cruiser, but not all of them together. As each high-cost item comes up for consideration, we know we could buy it and we are able to imagine how we would enjoy it. In this way we get some of the happiness of owning each item without actually doing so.

It is fundamental to the management of a business to have a business plan, yet how many of us bother with the same detail when it comes to our personal lives? We reduce what should be plans to hopes, and we go along looking for the lucky break.

CHAPTER 13 Obstacles Create Happiness

The obstacle principle ensures that there will always be enough obstacles in our lives to produce the happiness payoffs that are our due, and if those obstacles are not consciously created, they will be subconsciously created. Superficially, it may seem strange for us to go about setting obstacles for ourselves. The idea may be easier to accept by using terms such as goals, or plans or ambitions. Consciously created obstacles offer us a far greater degree of control over our lives to pursue what we enjoy rather than wait nervously to see what our subconscious serves up to us.

CHAPTER 14

Blame

> *It's not whether you win or lose,*
> *it's how you place the blame.*
> **Oscar Wilde**

Blaming is more than a game; it is a component of MA. When we wake each morning and look down the corridor of our intended short and long-term future, both planned and random, we imagine everything working out the way we want — even though our personal history tells us that won't happen. When there are disappointments, we use a mechanism as a panacea. It's called blame.

Certain noble people appear to accept personal blame when things go wrong. But that is actually a front. Nobody accepts blame. Okay, we made a wrong decision, and we were punished for it, but there is always a layer beneath that can reveal the reason we made the wrong decision. It was somebody else's fault.

Our power to reason leads us behind the scenery of what went wrong, enabling us to find out why. Nothing happens without a cause and if we peel back the responsibility layers, we will eventually come upon the one that shifts the blame away from us to another person, or an organisation or, as a last resort, bad luck.

As a child, my daughter would throw a tantrum when she was caught doing something naughty. Her response to our reprimand was to remind us that she hadn't asked to be born. That was the ultimate let-off for her. My wife and I had forced her into life and anything she did wrong was not her fault, but ours.

Many Asian countries hire motorbikes to tourists. If the tourist is unlucky enough to have an accident, the damage to the bike and anything else is usually his responsibility. It doesn't matter who was in the wrong; the bike shop is not interested. The hirer, (usually European) must pay up. Now this is not a case of intimidation by the bike shop to make a profit out of the hirer. It is how many Asians apply blame. Thai logic, for instance, says that if you did not have possession of the bike there could not have been an accident or subsequent damage. Clearly whatever happened is your fault simply because you were there.

My wife was in a parking station recently, patiently waiting for a car to drive out of a space so she could drive in. Another car in a space near her reversed without looking and ran into the rear of my wife's car. The driver jumped out in a rage and told my wife that if she hadn't been there, there would have been no accident. That was true of course, but illogical. The offending driver had quickly shifted the blame on to my wife. Of course, the insurance company sorted it out in the opposite direction, but the offending driver, an elderly woman, still believed in her innocence by moving the blame. The truth is, we all do that because it is part of MA. Sometimes we do it via an external declaration, but we always do it internally.

Most sporting contests have a winner and a loser. While the media traditionally relays the elation of the winner, the more riveting news interest is on the loser because that's where blame is generated most intensely, and we are attracted to witnessing it. If we were barracking for the losing side, and even though we didn't personally participate in the game, we feel some ownership of the loss. We want to see the blame being shifted away from our team losing. The referee is probably the most popular blame recipient, but there are many others like injury and sickness.

Blame has a secondary purpose, too. When blame is established, it often leads to compensation of some kind passing from the accused to the accuser. The law provides blame on a public scale and, once proven, usually involves recompense, either through a system of fines or compensation or paying a debt to society by being put in jail. In this sense, blame has the effect of being an achievement leveller in society.

In an earlier chapter, Crime and Punishment, we talked about how the creation of laws is an essential component of MA. Blame is the fuel that makes the law machine move. But unlike laws, which are imposed upon us, blame is a personal concept which exists continually in our thought process. And although the law needs blame to motivate it, much of our blame activity does not break or invoke any laws.

Like the discussion of other MA components, this is not a criticism, but identification. Blame is neither good nor bad. It simply is.

CHAPTER 15

Belief

Belief is not a matter of choice, but of conviction.
Robert Green Ingersoll

Fifty years ago, if a trusted friend had described to us the digital and computer era that we're living through now we wouldn't have believed it. And if that had been followed by an explanation of how computer viruses were created and spread, we would have laughed. How could machines catch viruses?

We all run along the belief rails that are built from our experiences. Some of those experiences are personally encountered while others are accepted or rejected simply on the statements of other people. They combine to provide us with the information on which to base our beliefs. Fifty years ago, we wouldn't have believed in computer viruses any more than we believe, or even understand, some of today's theories regarding quantum physics and the nature of the universe. Most of us don't bother to spend time on questions that call for belief unless they directly affect our everyday lives.

Belief comes from three sources: what we are told, scientifically provable facts, and supernatural phenomenon. MA imposes all three, but in widely varying proportions.

The most common source of belief comes from what we are told, especially if we trust the teller. The media peppers us with information which we quickly process to either believe or disbelieve. Mostly we believe, because we don't have the means to check what we are being told and we are too lazy to do so anyway. Moreover, believing what we are told has the added attraction of being easily repudiated if necessary. We often hear 'this didn't come from me, but I hear . . .' or 'I'm told that . . .' In fact, most of what we hear is true, which is why we have come to believe it. Information that we think is true gives us quite a shock when we discover it isn't.

Believing in scientifically provable facts might sound like a no-brainer but it is not, especially if it runs counter to opposing deeply held beliefs that may not be factually based. A case in point would be the explanation of creation. Those who believe that the biblical account is factually accurate, won't have a bar of the Big Bang which science tells us happened about 13.8 billion years ago.

Supernatural beliefs, whether in a deity, ghosts, new age, afterlife or a whole raft of non-physical phenomena are among the most powerful, simply because they exist beyond proof. They can even borrow from scientific logic. When a student asked my maths teacher at school how he'd arrived at a certain solution to an equation, the teacher would thunder 'Well, how else could it be?' If we translate that to the creation question, religious belief would tell us that there is no possibility other than via the hand of a deity. Based on that, we can then build a detailed impression of the deity, even to the interpretation of what the deity is thinking. And it could all be true. At the other end of the belief spectrum, we will find theoretical scientists who are convinced that something can come from nothing. Just because that doesn't make sense to us now, me included, does not make it untrue.

Still dealing with belief in the supernatural, religions and similar systems are festooned with a huge network of demands for carrying out what we might call secondary tasks. These are set down in rules and regulations, usually enunciated by senior clergy, to guide adherents on how to obey the demands of the belief and please the deity. They produce countless books and endless sermons on what the deity wants us to do — many of them contradictory — and then we have to decide which pieces of information to believe and which to reject — and how rigorously to do so.

Belief has a close family member: faith. The two are sometimes interchangeable, but faith calls for less hard evidence than does belief. While belief can sometimes crumble in the face of contrary evidence, faith can simply ignore it. Moreover, faith is a much more emotive concept than belief. We may debate somebody about a particular belief, but it is considerably more difficult to lock intellectual horns when our companion declares that, no matter what we say, he has faith.

Let's stop here before this becomes a discussion on what we should or shouldn't believe — because they are by-products. What we're identifying is a component of MA. Just like our need for hierarchies, we have a need, almost a compulsion, for belief. I'm tempted to suggest that belief is a psychological virus because it shares so much in common with love. But I'll leave that for another time.

While we can see the results of belief everywhere in our lives and those of others, we are much less aware of it as a part of MA. It is easy to mistake beliefs for the engine that induced them. On the surface, we might witness a number of events where there is enough common, convincing material for us to form a belief. As children, our parents may have taken us regularly to church where an obviously important man, up high in a pulpit, regularly told us about God, an intimately imagined entity in our lives who was behind many of the mysteries that confronted us. It is understandable why we become a believer, but the real issue here is that we had our unavoidable MA that obliged us to believe in something and we fastened onto God and all the accompanying trappings that our particular religion had added.

Religion is only one of many issues that can help satisfy our need to believe in the supernatural. Another is karma that had its roots in Buddhism, but is now a popular non-religious belief throughout the world. In essence it says that good deeds contribute to happiness, while bad deeds contribute to suffering. And just in case we try to turn karma into a current strategy, we are told that good or bad payoffs can take place in subsequent lifetimes. The 'golden rule' is another popular belief. Some people believe in democracy, or communism or the existence of spirits. Gambling and, in fact, all pursuits where luck is involved, is a disguised belief in the supernatural. The list of possible beliefs is huge and as variable as the number of people in existence. While there is a number of broad, definable categories, every individual's beliefs are different in content and combination. Like much of MA, we get the operating system, leaving us to fill in the content.

Beliefs are difficult to articulate because, although they may have a handy category heading, getting down to specifics can leave many people speechless. I experienced this recently when an atheist friend asked me if I believed in God.

'Tell me what you mean by God and I'll tell you if I believe,' I replied.

'I don't have to do that because I'm the non-believer,' he said. 'Non-belief is negative and irrefutable. That's the atheist position. So, again, do you believe in God?'

'I can't answer that with a simple yes or no,' I replied. 'How can I believe or disbelieve in something about which I have no scientific or personal experience — yet, anyway? I'm still trying to find out what God is. So far, my belief is that the universe was created by something, but I don't know what, and I'm prepared to accept that I don't have the knowledge to come to a conclusion. I'm quite happy with that.'

'Okay,' he said, 'you are in the agnostic club, which means that you believe there might be a god or there might not be.'

CHAPTER 15 Belief

And there our brief discussion ended, showing that belief can be positive, negative or neutral. Belief in God is a straightforward, popular category, but becomes very subdivided and scrambled once we get into detail. There are as many different versions of belief in God as there are people. MA obliges us to have belief, but we can decide what to believe in.

The old saying that 'the devil is in the detail' applies to our MA's demand for belief, because as soon as we proceed to the description of what we believe in, it becomes difficult, if not impossible to define. When pushed to descriptive limits, many people get angry or simply give up. They know what they believe, and live by it, and it works okay, so why threaten its stability with analysis?

As a fun exercise, try asking somebody what they believe in (I'd suggest you avoid religion) and then ask them to exactly define the ingredients of their belief.

Chances are they'd never bothered to do that and they will feel uncomfortable trying, especially when it comes to supernatural beliefs. The primary blockage is that they don't really know, in detail, what they believe in. It may well be that most people, if not all, are fundamentally agnostic when it comes to beliefs.

Leaving religion to one side, and going secular, we might

say: 'we believe that smoking is bad for our health.' That's a neat category, easy to understand and generally non-ambiguous. It sits comfortably as a core belief — which is why I don't smoke. But along comes a challenger. He asks what do we mean by smoking: cigarette, cigar, pipe, bong? Inhale or not? How often? How has our view changed since childhood? All of a sudden, we are not sure what we mean by smoking. Then when he moves on to good or bad health, what does that mean? The two major subjects here have become a sea of moving particles, some attached to one another, others discardable. While we still have the belief that smoking is bad for our health and we can assemble general information to back up our belief, it is difficult and uncomfortable to nail the definitive details as they apply to us, personally. The question becomes annoying. We know what we believe, so let's leave it at that, we mutter.

Many beliefs stand on feet of clay. And that doesn't really matter because we've responded to the MA demand for belief. The reasons are up to us. They can be right or wrong, and mostly we form beliefs on feelings and second-hand information rather than scientific evidence.

CHAPTER 16

Anger and Fear

Anger is just anger. It isn't good. It isn't bad. It just is. What you do with it is what matters. It's like anything else. You can use it to build or to destroy. You just have to make the choice.
Jim Butcher

You are frightened of everything. You call it caution. You call it common sense. You call it practicality. You call it playing the odds, but that's only because you're afraid to call it by its real name, and its real name is fear.
Mick Farren

Anger and fear are twin components of MA that are so common they get buried in the complex mix of what we are. Every day, every person (and possibly every animal) gets angry over something. In humans, it is because we think ahead of our actions in which we imagine the outcome we expect or want — and then it doesn't happen that way. Or it doesn't happen at all — which is even more annoying.

Anger can be fleeting or persistent. Its outcome can range between a passing irritation and a violent rage which may prompt a physical attack. It can be overt or covert. It can be expressed in words or actions or both. Even though a world without anger is often the expressed wish of the pious, it is one of those necessary counterbalances. The counterbalance to anger is elation. In truth, we don't want one to dominate the other. We're happiest with a mix of both.

MA has given us anger for several reasons. The main one is to ready us for battle and to diminish the likelihood of us being killed. Anger is accompanied by a physical release of testosterone as the stress level of the left hemisphere of the brain becomes more stimulated, accompanied by an increase in heart rate and arterial tension. While the physical manifestations of anger are well known, as are the mechanisms we use to control it (or, in some cases, fail to) its MA source is not acknowledged. While we can learn to control and harness anger to a degree, we cannot banish it from our lives. As with all other components of MA, it is neither good nor bad. It simply is.

CHAPTER 16 Anger and Fear

Along with anger comes a huge list of possible positive and negative outcomes. Using anger to save a loved one from harm is seen as positive. But striking somebody in anger, especially without warning, is seen as negative.

Anger has been an important ingredient in some of the greatest achievements and disasters in history. It is a powerful driver and can be added, like a chilli in a meal, to hot up the action.

I have anger to thank for my own far-reaching career move. In 1971, I was working in Melbourne as managing editor of one of Rupert Murdoch's magazines and had found my niche in life. The magazine was called *Australian Fashion News* and it covered the Australian apparel industry via a glossy, monthly trade publication. I was lucky to get the job because I wasn't highly qualified for it, but once I had started, I realised this was an occupation I was good at. It seemed that I had been placed on the earth to make magazines. Under my management and cheeky writing style, the magazine flourished. By year four, I was flying, but at that point Rupert decided he didn't want to be in trade magazines and sold *Australian Fashion News* to another company. I went with the package.

Under the new owner my wings were clipped. I had to provide reasons and get permission for everything I did, even though I had proven my trustworthiness and value to my previous employer — for years. My first year under the new owner became more irritating as it went along. I bought myself a company briefcase to carry a camera and papers on appointments with my advertising customers and editorial contacts. When I put in the expense claim it was rejected. That set off an intense examination of all my office expenses. I was told that I could now spend up to $10 a week unsupervised but any more than that would require pre-approval. I became angrier and angrier. Then I was told that, even though the magazine was still on a growth curve of revenue and popularity, another editor from the company was going to be sent in to 'help' me. I would have to share my office with him. The final straw was a curt note from head office in Sydney telling me that my small staff in Flinders Lane was consuming too many tea bags. I still remember vividly the day that memo arrived.

Anger drove me to quit the job, move interstate and start up my own fortnightly newspaper in opposition. I called it *Ragtrader* and I ran it for twenty profitable years before I sold it. If I hadn't been angry enough to rebel, my successful career move may never have happened.

We seldom acknowledge the role that anger plays in achievements. Somebody has something to prove. He or she has the machinery oiled and ready, but will often need to put a shot of anger into the fuel tank to achieve ignition.

CHAPTER 16 Anger and Fear

Another quality of anger is its ability to overcome fear and reason. When I was at school in Melbourne, I remember the day when a normally peaceful boy was baited by the school bully who broke his pencil and threw the pieces at his feet. The boy summoned so much anger that he put down his schoolbooks and downed the bully with a hail of punches that seemed to come out of nowhere. Like all of us, he had previously been frightened of the bully and if he'd resorted to reason he might have run away — which would have been the sensible thing to do. But anger overcame fear and reason. The outcome was what every witness wanted, but it might have gone the other way. The bully might have been a superior fighter and broken the aggrieved boy's nose as well as his pencil.

Because anger can overcome reason, it also shortens the delay before action. It works against patience. Anger is often impulsive. That is not say anger cannot be strung out over a period of time. In some cases, it can be smouldering and incremental, but this would apply to a situation where quick action is not an option. Anger demands resolution as quickly as practicable.

Anger and fear go hand in hand. If we are frightened, we will either look for protection and lay low or we will get angry and come out swinging. Sometimes we will alternate between the two. As long as a threat is intense enough, anger will nearly always overcome fear.

That brings us to another MA component, fear. Like anger, everybody experiences fear every day. It can be a fear of running late, or a fear of heights, or fear about some aspect of work. MA has given us fear to prolong our lives. It is telling us, in detail, what to avoid. Fear can be both practical and imagined. It is often difficult to tell the difference, especially if a fear is irrational. And even knowing it is irrational doesn't release us from it. I have a friend who has a fear of enclosed spaces. She cannot fly in the cabin of an aircraft or step into an elevator. She knows rationally that there is nothing to fear with either of these places, yet her fear persists. Psychological analysis might find out why she is frightened and that might release her from it, but that doesn't change the fact that fear is a perception, real or imagined, that danger is present.

Many components of MA are distorted by the individual, but that doesn't make them any less real.

If we acknowledge the MA directives of anger and fear we must look at the other sides of those coins, even though they don't have the same potency. In a strange way they are negatives. If we are not angry, we still may not be joyful. We spend most of our time in the middle ground between fear and joy. Right in the mid-point is quiet, unruffled equilibrium — a nice place to be. From that point we move to experience joy or fear depending upon what life serves up. While we want joy, we know it has little meaning unless we have the experience of fear. As we saw in the chapter about obstacles bringing happiness, endless joy is seductive, but is not a state we want to inhabit permanently.

The opposite of anger is not easy to define. It may also be joy, but again, we spend most of our time not feeling angry — but not necessarily joyful either. Perhaps the opposite of anger is something like equilibrium. I'll leave that one open for discussion.

CHAPTER 17

Questioning

*The most important thing is
to not stop questioning.*
Albert Einstein

We touched on this subject earlier but now I want to explore it as a stand-alone component of MA. We are again looking at a quality of human MA that is not shared by any other living creature on Earth.

A good murder mystery usually gives the reader plenty of facts and plenty of suspects. We join the detective as he or she tries to match the pattern of the facts to the suspects and invariably gets it wrong a few times before finally nailing the villain. Sometimes we crack the case before the detective does — much to our satisfaction. But how would it be if somebody had torn out the last five pages of the book and deprived us of 'who done it?' Our initial reaction would be annoyance in not knowing. Then, if we were really engaged with the story, we'd probably make up our own solution and move on to another book — hopefully with no pages missing.

This, of course, is trivialising quite a significant component of MA: the role of questioning, verbally, implied or internalised. Every statement of fact is preceded by a question. Immediately we are going to look for a statement that had nothing to do with a question. Let's discuss.

Imagine I'm walking into the clubhouse at my tennis club. I nod to a few people I know and then look out the window and say, 'we're in for a hot day.' Nobody asked me about the weather, so there was no question. Well, actually, there was. I asked myself, non-verbally, what I thought about the weather and I replied with a spoken statement. Nobody, unless deranged, simply 'comes out' with a statement unrelated to a question. MA dictates it can't happen.

MA provides us with this two-pronged conduit for progress. Even Sol, who probably talks to himself continually, would follow the question-and-answer MA obligation. Take it away and we all might as well be statues.

CHAPTER 17 Questioning

This question of questions has an interesting corollary to it. My channel tells me that there are only four possible answers to any question.

1. The correct, scientifically provable answer.
2. The well-intentioned but incorrect answer.
3. I don't know.
4. An intentionally incorrect answer.

While we all employ at least one of these answers to every question, sometimes we combine parts of more than one. We may give a correct answer and then add some incorrect information to it. But let's look at each of them as stand-alone answers.

The correct, scientifically provable answer is the most useful and satisfying. It is a favourite because it serves a purpose, aids progress and usually makes the giver of the answer feel good.

The well-intentioned but incorrect answer is little more than a guess. If it is accidentally correct, unintentional cause and effect has bailed us out. But it cannot be relied upon. In fact, it may lead to a disaster as in 'did you turn off the stove?' 'I think I did.'

'I don't know' is used more when there are minimum consequences attached to the answer or to throw up a smoke screen. It is really no answer at all. It is a transaction that confers a level of superiority on the questioner and ignorance on the answerer.

The intentionally incorrect answer is sinister because it is designed to mislead and deceive — usually for personal gain. People lose their lives based on these kinds of verbal transactions.

MA's role in all this is that it gives us four ways to answer any question, making us unique among living creatures. It is part of being human and enables us to anticipate the consequences of an answer to a question before we make it. Our anticipation may not turn out to be accurate and we may suffer for it, but we always have the choice.

CHAPTER 18

Addiction

*Addiction is not something we can simply
take care of by applying the proper remedy.
For it is in the very nature of addiction to feed
on our attempts to master it.*
Gerald May

Addiction is a component of MA. It can be defined as the repeated involvement with a substance or activity that occurs outside what is regarded by reasonable people as normal. That involvement may or may not be harmful. Immediately we have a problem over 'what is regarded as normal by reasonable people?'. Records of examinations by psychiatrists of their patients can be collated to give us a rough idea of abnormal behaviour, but it is still very subjective, tempered by the era and place in which the examinations are held. For example, the consumption of alcohol goes in and out of the normal band depending upon which country and time is under consideration.

There are good addictions, bad addictions and accepted addictions. Some bad addictions involve substances like nicotine or heroin, or the availability of psychological stimulants like pornography. And at the light end there are everyday habits that fall outside the average. If somebody drinks five glasses of wine over a week he is not regarded as an alcoholic, whereas the five glasses a day person is, and can be considered addicted. We may also ask if somebody who chooses to drink only water has an addiction too, which might be seen as akin to alcoholism. Maybe a more acceptable consideration might be of those who spend their lives devoted to prayer or even those whose religion demands they pray several times a day. Measured against the average (let's avoid the word 'normal') these people could be regarded as having an addiction — albeit a good or, at least, harmless addiction.

While we can usually identify the difference between good and bad addictions, how about accepted addictions? Let me give you the most obvious example: mobile telephones — that have now become smartphones. Because they are also miniature computers and cameras,

CHAPTER 18 Addiction

they offer the capabilities of recording, transmitting and receiving video and audio signals, storing personal information, retrieving general information from outside sources, carrying out calculations, watching movies, playing games and, I almost forgot, making telephone calls. Go to a bus stop or train station any morning of the week and we'll find most waiting travellers staring down at their smartphones. Likewise, people (especially young) dining together will often be paying more attention to their smartphones than to each other. Here we're looking at a powerful, accepted addiction. In fact, it is so accepted and widespread that it succeeds in disguising this addiction as a necessity.

Other popular and accepted addictions can be to shopping, washing, collecting, gaming and listening to music. They only identify themselves as addictions when they clearly exceed the average for no practical reason or are harmful to physical or mental health.

Everybody's behaviour falls outside the average, or 'normal' band in one way or another. In some cases, we have the choice of quitting the addiction; in others, not. Because addictions are not always visible to the observer, it doesn't mean they are not there. It simply means we don't know enough about the subject's behaviour. Even people who share an intimate relationship can miss each other's addictions, especially those which are considered bad, because they are the ones most likely to be hidden with the greatest care.

In an earlier chapter we talked about the MA component of judging ourselves by comparison with others. When we look at others, we are not seeing into them to discover their addictions. We therefore compare ourselves with false impressions of normality — which can lead us to the conclusion that we compare less favourably than we really do. People do not readily reveal their flaws.

Again, I make the point that by labelling addiction I am not criticising a component of MA. I am simply identifying it. We are all addicts in one way or another. The more harmful addictions are brought to our attention because they put people in danger or disrupt otherwise orderly lives.

CHAPTER 19

Revenge and Forgiveness

It is essential that justice be done, and it is equally vital that justice not be confused with revenge, for the two are wholly different.
Oscar Arias

By far the strongest poison to the human spirit is the inability to forgive oneself or another person. Forgiveness is no longer an option but a necessity for healing.
Caroline Myss

The pronouncements of many wise people send the message that revenge is to be resisted. Moreover, it is noble to resist revenge. Here are a few examples:

> *Revenge is like a ghost. It takes over every man it touches. Its thirst cannot be quenched until the last man standing has fallen.*
> **Vladimir Makarov**

> *In spite of the fact that the law of revenge solves no social problems, men continue to follow its disastrous leading. History is cluttered with the wreckage of nations and individuals that pursued this self-defeating path.*
> **Martin Luther King, Jr.**

> *In taking revenge, a man is but even with his enemy; but in passing it over, he is superior.*
> **Francis Bacon**

Revenge is saved-up retaliation. It is the intended return fire that is still in the breech of a gun after the battle is over. Revenge is a subsection of war, not necessarily a violent act, but intended to do harm to an opponent subsequent to a conflict. It comes under the broad category of 'unfinished business'. Most intentions and even plans to wreak revenge are never carried out. They either lose their motivation and slowly seep from our minds or we act them out in our imaginations to bring us some satisfaction and closure.

The fact that there is strong advice against revenge proves its existence and places it among the components of MA.

CHAPTER 19 Revenge and Forgiveness

The urge to revenge occurs to every person in varying degrees and is linked to the depth and frequency of the stress they are under. While revenge is very much part of the human behavioural mix, it appears to be rare in the MA of other living creatures. They tend to live in a more factual world, where what might look like revenge is really an act of protection or perceived threat. I doubt they hold grudges — although some would disagree with me.

Revenge can be active or passive. In some cultures, revenge killing is part of everyday life. Once one person has been murdered for a cause, it can set off a chain of revenge killings that can go on for years — sometimes centuries. The long religious conflict in Ireland delivered revenge killings on both personal and doctrinal grounds. Closer to home, gangland assassinations in Melbourne and Sydney always arouse fears that revenge will lead to more killings and perhaps involve innocent bystanders.

Passive revenge is more frequent because it is, frankly, easier. Say a processing clerk in the mail exchange is fired for no good reason that she can see. She believes that her job was essential to the smooth running of her department. She imagines that the department will now become a shambles and hopes that the manager who fired her will not only regret his action, but be punished for it, maybe by getting fired himself. Even though it probably won't go in that direction, the fired clerk hopes for passive revenge, and may even imagine that is what will happen, regardless of the real outcome.

Both active and passive revenge are often thwarted. Near the end of the Second World War millions of people wanted to carry out revenge against Adolf Hitler. The fact he was never found meant that revenge, no doubt via an execution, left all those people unfulfilled. Thwarted active revenge is difficult to handle and can produce psychological scarring.

Passive revenge is much more common. We all indulge in it. It too is an unavoidable component of MA. It may be driven by simple jealousy. In another chapter we talked about comparisons and how we feel when we don't measure up. One reaction is to bring the other person down rather than elevate ourselves. This is an act of revenge, a payback for being made to feel inferior. Although this usually takes the form of passive revenge, it can be active if the feeling is strong enough. Mindlessly damaging somebody else's property is often sparked by revenge, simply because it seems better than ours. We wouldn't expect those with beautiful, luxury cars to maliciously scratch somebody else's car. It would be far more likely to be carried out by those with a jalopy or no car at all.

Both active and passive revenge have an antidote that is evident in the three quotes above. The antidote for revenge is forgiveness. Somebody wrongs us, we feel the need for revenge but we resist it. So many religions preach the principles of forgiveness that we may be tempted to believe that, without religion, forgiveness would not exist. But all those religions have really done is to label another component of MA and claim it as their own invention.

We may well ask ourselves why we forgive. There are many reasons. One is that it is much easier than revenge, as well as being generally praiseworthy. That praise, it should be noted, has its limitations and is governed by contemporary community standards and expectations. We might be praised for forgiving our best friend when he threw up on our lounge or failed to appear at our wedding when he was the best man. But how would the crowd feel about forgiving the man who raped our daughter? In that case forgiveness might seem inappropriate while bashing his head with a hammer might seem praiseworthy — or at least understandable.

Forgiveness also has a darker side. Not only is it an easier way out, it also may be considered the coward's way out. Let's say we're sitting at a bar and a big, grizzly guy looks across and says our face reminds him of an arsehole. Revenge dictates we either trade insults or get into a fist fight. Forgiveness dictates that we ignore the insult, turn the other way and leave it at that. Thus, we go home without a broken nose and warmed by the glow of forgiveness. But did we take the coward's way out?

Although forgiveness comes from our MA, it is not compulsive, but rather optional. For that reason, it doesn't rank with revenge in its automatic application. An interesting side issue is forgiving oneself. It gets lumped in with forgiving other people but it is somewhat different. In order to forgive oneself we would either have to wipe the wrongdoing event from our memory or overlay it with compelling reasons as to why we should not have to bear the responsibility. We hold a kind of mental court, where the defence proves the case for not guilty. Often, we can forgive ourselves via blame that can include our upbringing, our bad luck or even our good deed that went pear-shaped. My own opinion is that we can never really forgive ourselves because of another major component of MA, guilt. We deal with guilt in the next chapter.

CHAPTER 20

Guilt and Remorse

*No guilt is forgotten so long as
the conscience still knows of it.*
Stefan Zweig

*Remorse ... is one of the many afflictions
for which time finds a cure.*
Winifred Holtby

We could be forgiven for thinking that guilt and remorse were one and the same, but they are more like first cousins. Guilt settles into the mind and is very difficult to eradicate, whereas remorse is shorter term and is eventually forgotten. They both begin, however, with 'I wish that hadn't happened.'

We create guilt when we behave unacceptably

— according to our own assessment, it must be emphasised. While that generally takes its cue from the laws under which we live, there are many exceptions. We may feel intense guilt over a divorce that we see as our fault, yet it is perfectly legal. Sexual matters are probably responsible for more guilt than other misdeeds; some legal and some illegal. In war times, soldiers can come away from a battle feeling guilt for having killed an enemy, even though they were following training and orders. Guilt varies with how we judge what we do in the light of our personal standards and beliefs.

Nowhere is guilt created more than in religion. Christianity specialises in it. Catholicism is probably the most guilt-rich of all branches, but gives its adherents an option for release through the process of confession and intercession. Guilt is not overtly expressed in religious teachings. It is not a sin, but rather a likely consequence of sin. Guilt doesn't have to be spelled out because those breaking religious rules are going to get a dose of guilt naturally. Religion has unconsciously found an effective way to trigger a component of MA — although it would never acknowledge that.

We are probably the only living creatures who suffer from guilt. It lies on our consciences like a rust spot on a piece of iron and is very hard to eradicate. Psychiatrists earn a large part of their living by helping their patients unload guilt. Of course, in some cases, we can go back and right a wrong, thus eliminating the original negative outcome and with it, the guilt. We can apologise, or return something we stole. This may be enough to neutralise the guilt and it may leave us — but only may. Guilt is unpredictable in ourselves and unreadable in others.

It should be noted that in the public arena guilt has a different function. The outcome of a criminal trial is usually a finding of guilty or not guilty. The trial has simply convinced a judge or a jury of the truth or otherwise of an accusation. In this case, the guilty may not feel guilt at all, especially if he or she was wrongly convicted.

In an earlier chapter we dealt with blame. Blame can be a catharsis for guilt. In this drug-laden age, it is not uncommon for a murder to be blamed on a powerful drug. The mistake the murderer made was in taking the drug in the first place, but can be forgiven (along with self-forgiveness) for the murder because the drug caused him to see the victim as the devil. The result is a more lenient sentence and maybe freedom from personal guilt.

Now let's talk about guilt's first cousin, remorse. It lies on the surface of consciousness and is shorter term than guilt. It is also easier to shed. We are far more likely to openly discuss remorse than we would guilt. We might describe remorse as self-anger and, like all anger, it subsides over time.

In recent years, a person found guilty of a crime can be sentenced more leniently if he or she shows remorse during the trial. That option only applies to those who have pleaded guilty. Convicted Australian drug smuggler Schapelle Corby maintained her innocence and therefore did not show remorse even though it cost her additional time in a Bali prison. Anybody who does not admit guilt obviously cannot show remorse for a crime they maintain they didn't commit.

Remorse has a far broader application than in criminal trials, of course. In commercial dealings we hear of 'buyer's remorse' when the purchaser regrets having made the purchase — but it's too late to cancel it. Saying sorry is another popular way of lessening the wrath of those who believe they have been wronged. In this scenario, we assume that saying sorry is prompted by remorse — although there are plenty of less noble reasons for saying sorry such as gaining political favour from the populace or avoiding getting our teeth knocked out in a pub when the angry big bloke takes offence at something we've said.

Fragmentary remorse (which we can also call regret), forms part of almost every day of our lives. We missed the train, we tripped over, we said something unnecessarily abrasive, we forgot a birthday, we were booked for parking. None of these events is going to have a serious impact on our lives but we still regret that they happened.

Remorse and regret are really degrees of the same MA component; one has a higher voltage than the other. Regret lasts a much shorter time than remorse and doesn't cut so deeply. Over time, a powerful remorse may settle in as guilt, and we're stuck with it.

CHAPTER 21

Luck

Shallow men believe in luck.
Strong men believe in cause and effect.
Ralph Waldo Emerson

We don't have to be gamblers to believe in luck. In fact, professional gamblers try to minimise luck by exercising a skill or a system intended to shut it down. But most people acknowledge the role of luck to some degree in their lives and the lives of those around them, even though it flies in the face of statistical and scientific evidence which tells us that there is no such thing as luck — only cause and effect. If we could know all the inputs that go into an event occurring, we would know the exact outcome in advance. But because, in most cases, total knowledge is not available, the outcome encourages us to believe in luck. This is not a black and white proposition, either. The so-called 'educated guess' is more likely to be right than a random pick, based on the logic that the more we know of the input, the better the accuracy regarding the result will be.

Luck can only be observed in retrospect. Although we may set up the conditions which we think will lead to an outcome we want, it is only after the event that we will know whether it worked for us or not. Winning the lottery once is regarded as lucky, twice seems even luckier. Both can be calculated as one in multiple chances. But that one chance must pre-exist, no matter how outlandish the odds. It would be possible to accurately predict the outcome of a lottery, but that would require the assembly of so much information, some of it undergoing continual change, that the task would become nonsensical and, for all practical purposes, not worth the trouble. It is so much easier, and lazier, to believe in luck and, at the same time, go along with the obligation that MA demands.

Prayer is related to luck when the deity is asked to make a certainty of that which is currently uncertain — like a promotion at work or nice weather for a wedding day. Asking the deity for a certain outcome is superficially asking that luck be taken out of the issue, but drilling down, it is actually asking the deity to interrupt the flow of cause and effect or suspend physics in favour of the person doing the praying.

Luck is not only connected to certain upcoming events but is also represented in symbols. Every culture has its lucky signs, colours, numbers and words. In some, religion and luck are intertwined. Many Asian cultures belief in Feng Shui, which concentrates on harmonising energy, and tries to shut out luck and replace it with cause and effect. To most westerners, Feng Shui is a difficult-to-understand ritual that is supposed to bring good luck, and they leave it at that. The fact is that Feng Shui is there to minimise luck.

Another branch of luck is superstition. In reality, superstition is also an attempt to take luck out of the equation. Before a motor race, a driver may have to put his left sock on before his right to obey a held superstition. Chinese people generally have a superstitious liking for the number eight. In scientific terms, numbers cannot affect outcomes, but if there is overwhelming popularity for certain numbers, or colours, or times, then they can exert market influence that has nothing to do with luck. Likewise, those espousing those popularities will assemble favourable examples to prove their beliefs.

If there is no such thing as luck why is it so deeply ingrained in us? Why do we continually wish ourselves and others good luck or, when things go wrong, do we so often attribute it to bad luck? The reason is that luck is part of MA. It can be suspended from our behaviour and replaced by scientifically based cause and effect, but it takes a lot of effort to do so. If we want to suspend luck in our lives, we must continually pursue the truth of cause and effect and remind ourselves of it daily. Most of us simply can't be bothered going to all that trouble.

So far as we can tell, humans are the only living creatures conscious of luck. If there are superior life forms to ours elsewhere in the universe, they probably don't believe in luck because their understanding of cause and effect would negate the idea of luck.

CHAPTER 22

Ownership

The instinct of ownership is fundamental in man's nature.
William James

Since awareness is confined to the time period of our lives, ownership is also limited to that brief period. Therefore, at best, we are only temporary custodians of assets. Very rich people, when near death, could be forgiven for feeling resentful that their pile of wealth will soon go to other people who didn't earn it and probably don't deserve it. Immediately after our last breath, we own nothing. This, of course, ignores the possibility of an after-death conscious state, because we don't have reliable evidence of its existence. But what we do know is that the dead don't have any control over what they used to own.

A recent movie called *The Aftermath* touched on the ownership of property when the British occupied the heavily bombed German city of Hamburg after having won World War Two. The question arose, although never answered, as to who owned a certain stately German mansion during occupation. The pre-war owner, a German architect, had to hand over his house to a British colonel who graciously allowed him to stay on in the attic. By winning the war, did the allied forces now own Germany and everything that was in it, including the people and what they could produce? And if they did own it all, how would they divide the spoils? Moreover, how many of the conquering country's citizens would want to move to another country simply to occupy property at the expense of its vanquished former owners who now would have nowhere to live? Again, assuming the allies controlled and owned all of Germany the day the surrender was signed, was that ownership permanent? History has shown that it was not, that Germany was divided, then unified, then allowed to become one of the richest nations on Earth — all in less than fifty years. It points to the fact that there is an MA component of intrinsic ownership — although we may suspend or even deny it for a time.

Even though ownership does not operate either side of the lifetime of the 'owner', it seems real for the duration of his or her awareness. We are programmed to want to 'own' not just physical property, but any identifiable notion to which our senses respond. We may lay ownership to an idea, a song, a fragrance, an interpretation, a view or a copyright. That ownership may or may not be provable at law, but it doesn't really matter. What does matter is that ownership is a component of MA and must be taken into account when we're considering our behaviour as a species.

Ownership is a stabilising factor in the ups and downs of living. It is the physical and theoretical nest to which we return. While it is more highly developed in humans because of our awareness complexity, we are not alone among living creatures whose MA obliges them to sense and defend ownership. A bird will defend the ownership of its nest, or a cat its territory. Ownership can be very short or it can be lifelong. Much of what is considered owned has a time limit on it. Most higher functioning living creatures move in and out of habitats, owning them for a while and then abandoning them. They also lay ownership to the small space which they occupy and usually some of the space around it as well. If that space is 'invaded' there is trouble because their ownership has been threatened.

When the British claimed ownership of Australia in 1788, the Aborigines didn't know that they no longer owned Australia — according to British law anyway.

Furthermore, it is doubtful whether the Aborigines ever contemplated national ownership; there was no need and no point. The question of who owns Australia now is somewhat awkward. From the original British and then Australian government position of total ownership by non-indigenous Australians there has been a steady drift back to Aboriginal ownership marked by the historic Mabo decision in 1992 and the subsequent Native Titles Act of 1993 which gave substantial land 'back' to the Aborigines — and is still doing so. Since then, there has been a quiet groundswell of recognising Aboriginal 'traditional' ownership of all Australian land. An increasing number of public and private gatherings begin with a statement acknowledging traditional Aboriginal ownership of the land upon which the gathering is being held. The word 'traditional' serves as notional protection against the land being righteously seized by so-called indigenous Australians and the occupants having to move on — possibly out of Australia.

When we become engaged by the question of who owns Australia, we are really being distracted by the playing out of an MA imperative rather than looking at the bigger picture. One MA component is our need to claim ownership even though, in reality, it exists purely in the imagination. It is estimated that the Aborigines were present in Australia between 40,000 and 60,000 years before European 'invasion' — which equates to ownership before that. But who came before the Aborigines? Because Australia was once joined by a land bridge to New Guinea (and Tasmania was part of the mainland) it is highly likely that other races preceded the Aborigines as occupiers. If so, what happened to their ownership? If we keep going back in the evolution of homo sapiens, we end up in the water as jellyfish and can ask ourselves the same question: What did we own then? Thus, the concept of territorial ownership becomes absurd and illustrates that it is no more than a perception. But, as we know, we live in a world of perception. Ownership is part of it, so we accept it. What we can say in summary is that ownership doesn't exist in reality, and that the MA perception of ownership only applies while the owner is alive and aware.

Ownership comes with its own ignition system: desire. Ownership can only exist after desire is created. We might think there is a contradiction to this if ownership is thrust upon us, unbidden, like a remote uncle dying and leaving us his valuable stamp collection. We may have never desired the collection or even known about it. But once we find out about the inheritance, the test of desire is applied. While we may now legally own the stamps, we may not desire them. That could lead to disposing of the stamps because we desire money more than the collection, or leaving them in a cupboard as legally owned but not owned in the MA sense. This illustrates the fact that ownership is an MA component rather than a legal definition.

CHAPTER 23

Ritual and Symbol

There is a comfort in rituals, and rituals provide a framework for stability when you are trying to find answers.
Deborah Norville

Symbols are powerful because they are the visible signs of invisible realities.
Saint Augustine

Like many MA directives, ritual is so ingrained in our everyday lives that we are hardly aware of its presence. We notice ritual most when we are observers of precisely planned events that are not part of our regular routine. We both expect and create ritual to add weight and importance to an event. It can involve how we dress, what we say, how we move — mostly to a prearranged routine. While ritual is not the event itself it can assume greater importance.

For instance, a birthday is simply a mathematical calculation measuring one year of time, yet the ritual of celebrating a birthday is important and, in its various forms, almost universal. When you think about it, the celebration would be more logical directed to the mother who, after all, did all the birth work. Some people now celebrate the day they were conceived, thus bringing the role of fatherhood into the ritual.

Probably nothing employs ritual more than religious events. If you were a regular attendee of Jewish religious services and one day found yourself siting in a pew at a Catholic mass your most arresting impression, and maybe incredulity, would be of ritual. Even though the Jewish service would be full of its own ritual, it would have become unremarkable because you had grown used to it. But the Catholic service would immediately get your attention and perhaps curiosity, mostly because of ritual. You may acknowledge the same deity at the top of both hierarchies, but the worship ritual is dramatically different. Similar reactions would apply to observing other, unfamiliar religions.

Some other activities that are draped in ritual would include legal proceedings, coronations, weddings,

CHAPTER 23 Ritual and Symbol

funerals, graduations, sporting events, down to shaking hands and standardised greetings. Virtually every group activity is embellished by ritual. If it is repeated often enough it acquires the quality and annotation of tradition. As such, it largely escapes the need to explain its value or even its purpose.

We are not trying to downplay or ridicule ritual. We love much of it and acknowledge its importance in satisfying us as to the veracity of the event we're witnessing. We must acknowledge that, to humans, ritual has value. It is a case of perception overriding reality, because if we strip away the ritual, we don't delete the event. Of course, we could argue that ritual is intrinsic to the event and that might be right. But we cannot have ritual without a core event for it to embellish.

Other living creatures on Earth seem to indulge in ritual too, although it seems more outcome-driven than the human use of ritual. A male lyrebird shaking his startlingly beautiful fan of tail feathers looks to be ritualistic, but it has a direct purpose in attracting a female lyrebird for mating. Elephants seem to have rituals, especially when one member of the herd dies and the survivors exhibit behaviour that many observers have interpreted as ritual mourning.

Like most modes of human behaviour, there is an

acceptable amount of ritual based on community expectations or religious laws, but when this is exceeded it becomes an obsessive-compulsive disorder. In Judaism, for instance, there are several occasions when ritual hand washing is required, but when a person washes his or her hands continually, it falls into the disorder category.

It is worth acknowledging that many rituals grew from practical necessities which became unnecessary over time but have remained as ritual, some transforming into tradition — which then needs no justification.

Symbols, which we could say are a first cousin of rituals, fall into two categories.

One is a component of MA and the other is unrelated to MA. The type of symbol that is closely associated with ritual (and therefore a component of MA) could be called the signposts of ritual. When I was in primary school in Melbourne, the students would assemble every Monday morning in the quadrangle to salute the Australian flag. The words spoken and the actions taken were ritual. The flag itself was a symbol. The material from which a symbol is made seldom has any bearing on its impact. A little paper flag invokes just as much patriotism as a big textile flag. It is what humans attribute to the symbol that gives it importance and identifies it as a component of MA.

CHAPTER 23 Ritual and Symbol

Certain statues, in particular those that are related to religion, are powerful symbols. To Australians, so is the slouch hat worn by its 'digger' soldiers. Examples of other powerful symbols are the Jewish Star of David, the Christian cross, the bull and bear images to illustrate the stock market or the interlocking shapes of yin and yang.

The other types of symbols have not come from MA but are communicating signs or instructions. They have nothing to do with ritual either. Instructive symbols can be identified by their ability to be substituted for words. For instance, an arrow could be substituted for the words 'this way' or a red hexagon for the word 'stop'. We see a lot of instructive symbols on building construction sites, roadworks and messages to car drivers. We also see them in more technical roles in science, with the likes of chemical and mathematical symbols. We use instructive symbols because they convey a message more quickly than words and do not depend on language. These types of symbols are the result of human reasoning and logic rather than a component of MA and they are far more common. In fact, so much so, that we hardly notice them, even though we use and read the relevant ones every day.

Some instructive symbols identify a product or company. The symbol for Apple electronic products is one of the most unmistakable in the world. It immediately tells us who designed and manufactured the product. Some symbols take the form of logos that spell out a company name, like Coca-Cola.

CHAPTER 24

Imagination

Every great advance in science has issued from a new audacity of imagination.
John Dewey

Does a dog imagine? We know he has preferences for certain foods, for being taken for a walk, for some people more than others, for fetching a ball. Given the opportunity he will mate, sniff and pee on posts, run and wag his tail. And if we observe him asleep, we will see that his twitches indicate that he dreams. But what part does imagination play in his life? Because we can't get inside a dog's mind, we can't tell whether he imagines or not. He certainly desires, and he certainly reacts to stimulus, and he certainly sums up what he observes and acts upon it, but when he is not occupied dealing with current events, does he imagine future outcomes?

The answer is, we don't yet know — although animal psychologists have come up with some interesting research. Animals play, dream and develop tools for gathering food, which would indicate that they do exercise imagination. What we know for certain is that MA bestows intense imagination upon us. In order to be able to imagine, we first have to have knowledge to give us the essential building blocks. But there is no point having a stack of blocks, and by attaching them at random, hope to make something useful — unless you claim it as a work of abstract art and charge a fortune for it. Imagination, courtesy of MA, provides a blueprint, sometimes clearly defined and sometimes not, of a new hypothesis or product. In many cases, we don't have the blocks necessary to assemble the new hypothesis or product. Imagination leaves us with a destination but not the means to get there — yet.

Before the beginning of the twentieth century there were no airplanes — as in heavier than air machines that could leave the ground. Although many people in the nineteenth century would have imagined a flying machine, the building blocks were not available. By 1902, still buoyed by imagination, the Wright Brothers assembled the required building blocks and produced

CHAPTER 24 Imagination

the first airplane. That, in itself, became a building block to be joined to the development of better propulsion engines, construction materials, knowledge of weather, navigation, and all the other items that have gone into producing today's jet aircraft. They now become one of the building blocks and are joined by others that are pointed at the next creation of imagination related to transport. This is a cart before the horse process, because imagination precedes realisation. A new hypothesis or product has first to be imagined before the assembly of building blocks can begin.

Most people think of Albert Einstein as a physicist and mathematician, but he was much more than that. He delved into religion, philosophy and ethics. In his book *Cosmic Religion: With Other Opinions and Aphorisms* he said 'imagination is more important than knowledge. For knowledge is limited, whereas imagination embraces the entire world, stimulating progress, giving birth to evolution. It is, strictly speaking, a real factor in scientific research.'

While we can look at imagination as a gift from MA, we must also regard it as an unavoidable compulsion. Like hierarchies, imagination is simply the way MA dictates how we go about one aspect of living. Imagination differs from other MA components in that it does not require the presence of other people to activate it. Our friend Sol would surely have imagined his cave more comfortable or his ability to catch fish more efficient. Over time, with the right building blocks, he might have imagined and come up with a fish net.

I'm thankful for imagination because it has enabled me as a writer. But I don't feel privileged, because every other person on Earth has, and exercises, imagination.

One of our weaknesses as a species is the flimsy division between imagination and memory. Once an event has passed, we are left with the memory of it. If we want to recall that memory, maybe as a vital element in a legal matter, or as the basis for an important decision, its accuracy becomes critical. In some cases, our effort to remember flips across to imagination and when that happens it can bring disastrous results. Although they can operate side by side, memory and imagination come from two different sources. Memory is a function of the brain and is stored in the hippocampus, the neo-cortex and the amygdala. Imagination is a component of MA and is not stored anywhere because it requires spontaneity to bring it into existence.

Let's consider the sequence that leads to invention. It runs: information (from memory or outsourced) fed into imagination, leading to a search for components, leading to assembly, leading to invention. Because of the obstacles along the way, the outcome of imagination only rarely leads to invention. But that doesn't change the hard and fast rule that invention must always be preceded by imagination. Our problem as a species is that while we continually exercise imagination over a broad range of challenges and issues, some basically mechanical and others purely fantasy, we hesitate to get out the building blocks and to create an invention, whether it's for a new form of energy or a better screwdriver. Once again this is part of our MA. We take in an overwhelming number of bits of often unrelated information for our imagination to play with, and then direct it to select and assemble some of those bits so they become an invention. The rest simply dissolve.

CHAPTER 25

Expectation

> We must rediscover the distinction between hope and expectation.
>
> **Ivan Illich**

My *Adam Exx* trilogy, which I've mentioned previously, was based on the concept of expectation. Adam was the first man on Earth — although he didn't realise it. Unlike the biblical Adam, my Adam lived in a world created by his expectations. He was an experiment by a higher intelligence that wanted to know how a human — which it had created — would develop if left entirely uninfluenced by anything outside it. To facilitate this, whatever Adam expected, would be made real. Thus, he lived in a world of his own creation. To find out what happened to him you'll have to read the books, but copy sales is not the reason I'm recounting this story. Expectation was a component of Adam's MA, but in this case his creators had the technology to instantly turn those expectations into reality.

The concept is, of course, fictional. In the lives we lead, only some of our expectations work out exactly how we visualise them while the rest deliver us various degrees of disappointment. And let's not forget the third state, which sometimes thrills us and sometimes devastates us: the unexpected. Somebody dies for no logical reason, we win a lottery, the company we work for goes bust, we crash our car, the dud goldmine we have shares in strikes a mother lode. There is no doubt that the unexpected is a major spice of living. It is not part of MA but rather the outcome of an infinite matrix of cause and effect. We dealt with that in the chapter about luck.

The Ivan Illich quote above is relevant to understanding expectation. Imagine standing in front of a door labelled Expectation One. When we open it, we find the expectations we might call certainties. For instance, when we wake tomorrow morning, we would expect to be in the bed we went to sleep in the night before, to be in our bedroom, to have the bed covers over us that were there last night. When we get up and our day begins,

CHAPTER 25 Expectation

there are more 'certainty' expectations. Our breakfast ingredients are still where we left them in the cupboard yesterday morning.

Now there is another door. Only most of what lies behind that door is going to fulfil our expectations, too. It might be to do with work, interactions with people or even the traffic conditions on the commute to work.

The third door will start to show a few expectations that don't work out. The payment that was due to us didn't arrive. The appointment to lunch was cancelled. Probably none of these failed expectations are too serious and we ride over them. Some expectations of failure may turn into success, too. The tender we expected would fall short of the brief we were given, unexpectedly succeeds.

There is now a succession of doors, each a bit further from home and each more advanced in time. Eventually, there is one behind which none of our expectations succeed. Don't be alarmed, we are not facing annihilation, because we've already passed through many doors where our expectations have been fulfilled, so life is still okay.

Now for the last door. There are no expectations there. We've run out of them, but now we have a new sub-component of expectation: hope. The Online Dictionary. com defines hope as 'the feeling that what is wanted can be had or that events will turn out for the best'. When expectation gets the wobbles, it morphs into hope. With hope there is also a series of doors, representing degrees of likelihood. If we hope our team wins on Saturday, that has more likelihood attached to it than if we hope our ticket wins the lottery. Eventually hope fades into absurdity as in hoping we will live for two hundred years.

Both expectation and hope are intangibles, even though we may allocate percentage likelihoods to them. They are feelings we have, empirical estimates we make. They are a component of MA. Although many other living creatures also get expectation from their MA, I doubt that they experience hope. Does a female cat that comes into season hope a tom will climb over the fence and mate with her? Maybe we could define that as hope but it is more likely to fall into the category of an expectation that may or may not be fulfilled.

CHAPTER 26

Dressing

Style is a way to say who you are without having to speak.
Rachel Zoe

Since a substantial part of my working life has been spent writing about the fashion industry, I understand the significance of style in dressing. Every new season brings with it a whole lot of new reasons to dress in a different way. Colours change, silhouettes and shapes change, fabrics change and, nowadays, there are peripheral influences like ethical production, sustainability and the moral question of throwing away clothing that is not worn out or, in some cases, not worn at all.

Observers looking in from outside the fashion industry

might conclude that designers make their living — and some of them a very lucrative living — by seducing innocent, childlike consumers with 'something different' that encourages them to throw away perfectly good clothes and buy new ones. Some would regard that as immoral, casting designers in a bad light.

Before I bring MA into the argument, let me define what a fashion designer is. He or she has the gift of interpretation. As we saw in the chapter on artistry, art comes into existence when something is expressed in a form different to the original. For example, a human body expressed in paint on a canvas; lost love expressed in a poem; an abstract idea expressed in a sculpture. A fashion designer is also an artist when he or she expresses the changing whims and convictions of society in clothing.

Take it from me, there are plenty of unsuccessful designers, just like there are plenty of unsuccessful interpreters in all forms of art. Simply put, those who flop have not moved into parallel with the changing whims and convictions of the masses, their customers. The public processes, largely unconsciously, what is going on in the world and buys clothes that correspond to its feelings. This is a massive, highly complex process that is currently beyond measurement but it is the relationship that is responsible for purchases, not only of clothing, but most consumer goods in which design plays a key role.

CHAPTER 26 Dressing

Cars are similar to clothing when it comes to fashion. Their primary purpose — transportation — is now a given and plays second fiddle to shape, colour, add-on gadgets and the overstated importance of safety.

It must also be acknowledged that certain people have the ability to influence the whims and convictions of the masses. The internet blogger with thousands of followers can create popularity for almost anything. But bloggers (currently known as 'influencers') are just one part of the mix of factors in decisions to purchase. They line up with politics, wars, crimes, sports, music, travel, food — the list is immense. And note that the artistic contents of this list interact with one another. The fashion designer expresses them in clothing. The motivation behind this is that MA dictates we dress, as well as acquire, many other consumer products to express an opinion and identity.

That opinion and identity will be individually sourced but then find common ground with others. The MA imperative is to partly align with like-minded people and partly to present an individual picture to the world. Thus, no two people will dress identically, unless by agreement — such as being a member of a team or regimented group like an army.

Although we might turn up odd exceptions, animals do not share this part of MA with us. Their changes of appearance are functional — either for protection, hunting or mating. Chameleons, for example, change their colour to disguise themselves from predators. Unlike us, animals are not driven to make statements about themselves by changing the appearance of their outer covering.

We might question why some people dress in shapeless, dull clothes whereas others add to their impact with what they wear. And we might conclude that people either care about how they look, or they don't. Although it is often subconscious, everybody is aware of how they look, or intend to look — and that is largely expressed in how they are dressed. What we pick from our drawers and wardrobes every morning is always intentional. If we look terrible or we look attractive, that is what we want our appearance to be.

As an interesting point, we might consider the evolution of dressing as an indication of the evolution of MA. Originally our species wore animal skins for bodily protection. That developed into a secondary role of gender delineation. As soon as the animal skin was given a shape to flatter the human body, or it was changed in colour, the fashion industry was born.

CHAPTER 27

Networking

Networking is not about hunting. It is about farming. It's about cultivating relationships. Don't engage in 'premature solicitation'. You'll be a better networker if you remember that.
Ivan Misner

Although the internet has given it a great boost, networking was well into its ascendency as a recognised tactic, especially in promoting business, long before the advent of the internet. In essence, it goes back to MA.

Like many other components of MA, networking requires there be more than one person. Solitary Man has no use for it. But, unlike hierarchies or systems that can have a long lifespan, networking forms and, just as quickly, reforms. Let's say we walk into a room full of strangers at a party. A few drinks having freed up shyness, people introduce themselves to one another and begin the filtration process of who is of interest and who is not. That can be based on who is informative, influential, amusing, sexually attractive, among many attributes that we look for when meeting people. Even those we know come in for regular reassessments. Networking is like making a thumbnail sketch of everybody we see, adding impressions and information to it and deciding whether to attempt to spend time with that person or move on to another. This produces a confusing matrix, but it must satisfy us because we repeat the process over and over, not just at a party but every time we are in the company of other people.

Even if we decide to be a wallflower at the party and sit alone in a corner, networking continues — albeit at a lower intensity.

Networking is far from exclusive to human MA. All animals, and probably some plant life, engage in networking. Have you ever looked in on a dog minding centre and observed the networking that goes on with a room full of dogs? They could almost be people, judging by the way they behave.

CHAPTER 27 Networking

Like many components of MA, networking is so deeply ingrained into our behaviour patterns that it has become almost invisible. We just do it.

Speech is simply part of the machinery of networking. Certainly, it is an important part, probably the most important, but networking does not live or die by speech.

Another part of the networking machinery is the compulsion to belong to a one or more organisations. The most fundamental of these is family. Then there is the club, the company, the informal drinking group, the society, the professional association, the religious congregation. The examples are vast, and the reasons why these affiliations are formed is for the purpose of networking among their members more than serving the cause that has brought them together. An ignorant observer might think that the purpose of the people who drink together at the pub is to consume alcohol. But drinking is only the moderator of the real purpose of networking.

Networking can also spring from impersonal sources. We see this particularly in public rallies where people are drawn together for a cause, often with a political mainspring. The sometimes-violent protests against mainland China's threatened changes in Hong Kong's criminal procedures produced networking on a massive scale as people, most of whom did not know each other, were linked by a common need to network.

We might also be tempted to identify communication, in its many forms, as a stand-alone component of MA but again it is also a part of networking. In fact, we could say that communication is a synonym for networking — as long as we agree that it is an MA imperative.

CHAPTER 28

Systems

Systems and processes are essential to keep the crusade going, but they should not replace the crusade.
Simon Sinek

Because a certain amount of common behaviour is essential to the working, in fact survival, of the human race to the point where it seems instinctive, we shouldn't assume that it falls outside MA. I'm talking about systems. They can also be described as routines, habits or behavioural patterns.

Every hierarchy is a system, but not every system is a hierarchy. One of the simplest definitions of a system is "an organised or established repeating procedure". From that, we might ask, organised by whom or established by whom? And the answer is MA. Unless MA directed us to build systems for so much of what we do, we would descend into chaos and not survive for very long.

Let's leave humans aside while we look at a beehive. If ever you wanted to find a naturally occurring system, there it is. The hive system, which is agreed upon and carried out by all the bees without dissention, ensures their survival, even though we steal their honey. Where did the bees get their system? The answer is from their MA. It is not clear whether each bee's MA is identical or whether the MA varies according to the occupation of the bee. The overarching principle is that all living creatures that have a mind, are directed by MA. While we accept that a horse has a mind, and therefore MA, we might ask whether a tree has a mind. It probably does, because it has to make decisions about nutrition, growth and reproduction. They come from a mind nothing like our own, but a mind nonetheless, and directed by MA.

The devoutly religious may say that we act in the way that God set up for us, and that although we have the choice to do good or evil, the systems that make our life work are a heavenly gift. I suppose they are, if we want to believe that God created MA for all life forms. As I've said before, I won't argue against a creator of some kind, but I have trouble in accepting the sometimes trite, unimaginable or unlikely explanations offered by many religions. Like physicist and broadcaster, Professor Brian Cox, I'm content with 'we don't know'.

We ought to visit Sol when considering this question. Although he has no use for systems that involve interaction with other people, he has certainly constructed his own systems, mostly to do with gathering food for his survival. He may also have systems to do with protecting himself from the unfriendly bears that might wander into his cave at night.

Systems come into being in the way that hierarchies do. When people gather, their MA directs them to create systems. The bigger the gatherings the more systems there are. Some systems are backed by laws to make sure they are observed and operated. The monetary system is a prime example. My channel's definition of money is that it is power in reserve. It is therefore valuable as a common denominator that can we apply to satisfy most of our needs. The very idea of money itself goes back thousands of years and replaced bartering. Today we still use money — although it is being steadily moved into a digital form — to store power which can be turned into the ability to act. It is one of our most complex systems, and essential for the functioning of society. While it is a directive from MA, money is also one of the few systems that is not evident in any other living creature. Birds, for example, have possessions, but they have no system that gives them a monetary value so that their possessions can be bought or sold.

Apart from general systems, like money, we each are part of a multiplicity of personal systems. Our family has its systems, so does our work, our hobbies, even our bodily functions. Our lives are so full of systems, many of them overlapping and some opposing one another, that we may not see them as a separate imposition of our MA. Like the air we breathe, we mostly only acknowledge its existence when it is absent. In the case of absent air, we immediately fly into survival mode and fight to stay alive, whereas most of our systems give us time to adjust, create or delete.

While some systems are subject to laws, most are not, and are simply abandoned when something better comes along. The manual system of individually weighing and bagging sugar and flour when doing the household shopping was abandoned because of pre-packaging and supermarkets. Now online services offer the alternative system of not even having to visit physical shops.

MA propels us towards systems in almost every pursuit in life and provides us with the ability to neglect them

CHAPTER 28 Systems

when it suits us. Many of them become tales that grandfathers tell to amuse children.

A ruling factor about systems is that they always decay and are replaced by new systems. This has a lot do with another component of MA: change. An established system is an open invitation for change. We spoke of our monetary system earlier. Yes, we still use the concept of wealth expressed in monetary terms, but the system employing gold and banknotes is changing into numbers recorded on electronic machines. Systems like this work as long as people believe in them — which brings in another component of MA we've discussed: belief.

The paragraph above has prompted me to point out another example of how MA components interact with one another. Here we have systems, change and belief all swirling around together. Sometimes they conflict, leading to a battle that goes on largely in our subconscious.

CHAPTER 29

Uniqueness

*Always remember that you are absolutely unique.
Just like everyone else.*
Margaret Mead

An important part of what we are is how we internally view ourselves, and that usually contrasts with how other people see us. We seldom speak truthfully of how we see ourselves because we know too much and we don't want to announce our shortcomings for fear that would make us vulnerable and damage our public image. So, with the exception of sessions with our psychiatrist, we mostly keep schtum.

However, there is one component of MA dealing with our

internal view of ourselves that is common to everybody and scientifically factual. It is our uniqueness.

So far as we can tell, uniqueness applies to everything in the universe. Perhaps we should qualify this by acknowledging that uniqueness only comes into being when atoms combine to make a variety of complex structures. Below that level, everything in the universe is the same. So, to bring MA into the discussion, let's agree that our starting point is atomic complexity.

Every snow pattern is unique, every fingerprint, every face, every blade of grass, every cloud. Have you ever sat on the seashore watching waves breaking and realised that no two are the same or ever will be? We are surrounded and overwhelmed by uniqueness. It applies to every event as well. Legendary cellist, Pablo Casals said 'each second we live is a new and unique moment of the universe; a moment that never was before and never will be again'.

Saying that every person is unique is stating the bleeding obvious, but MA makes sure that we take the uniqueness of everything in the world around us and apply it to how we see ourselves as well. Although we may conform to behavioural patterns and march in step with the rest of the army for purely practical reasons, our internal view of ourselves is quite different.

CHAPTER 29 Uniqueness

MA imposes upon us the continual reminder that goes something like this: there is nobody like me; I am unique to the point where people who observe me don't know who I really am. Only I know — and sometimes even that can be puzzling.

Uniqueness is a two-edged sword. People who achieve greatness in any field of endeavour have to be more radical than the rest, otherwise they could not become prominent. The same goes for people who operate outside the laws that the majority has created. Whilst they are seen as loathsome rather than great, they still stand out from the crowd. Between the extremes of good and bad behaviour is a whole gradation of uniqueness that falls outside the average. We might call it eccentric, interesting, stimulating, or outrageous, and we may approve or disapprove of it.

We each keep our uniqueness largely under wraps because a certain amount of conformity is necessary for survival and tribal acceptance. But our inner mental workings, thrust upon us by MA to continually acknowledge our uniqueness, are quite different. How we act and what we say can be at extreme odds with what we think.

Our personal view of our uniqueness is not static, either. The way we perceive ourselves changes by the minute as does our perception of other people and the world at large. The whole setup is fluid. The self-perception of the person who goes to bed tonight and the world in which he or she lives, will not be the same tomorrow morning. We continually reset, sometimes minutely and sometimes broadly. We only ever visit places and people once in a particular place and time frame. But through all this continual change of perception, we stick to the MA core belief that we are each unique.

CHAPTER 30

Enough is Enough

*When it's time for me to walk away from something,
I walk away from it. My mind, my body,
my conscience tell me that enough is enough.*
Jerry West

While the term 'enough is enough' comes up in everyday conversation, it is also one of MA's most frequently engaged components. And like all MA components, we each have a unique dosage, leading to our own estimate of how much is 'enough'. We are much better at defining when we don't have enough. People dying of starvation obviously know they are not getting enough food. On the other hand, obese people are probably getting more than 'enough' food.

In most cases, our concept of 'enough' is untrustworthy. Neither is it fixed. What was once enough may no longer be enough. Comparisons with the assets of other people will influence what we believe is enough for ourselves and others. Our MA will always present us with the need to personally and continuously estimate how much is enough, but we should examine the quantities prior to adopting them. While it is impossible to prevent MA saddling us with this component, the real issue is how we deal with it. Misinterpretation, for example, leads the already obese person who continues to eat excessively, into threatening his or her health and life. Likewise, the anorexic is being self-deceived in the 'enough' stakes by wanting to eat less to become thinner.

The 'enough is enough' question can be represented as a fork in the road. One side leads to absolutely 'enough' while the other leads to accepting that we cannot get enough of what we want, but we'll make do with what we've got - for the time being. While that might give us temporary peace of mind, it doesn't stop us from continually looking up the other fork just in case some new opportunities have opened up there.

Let's consider a few examples, beginning with wealth. The acquisition of net worth is an almost universal desire. I say 'almost' to preclude individuals who have, through internal decision, consciously chosen poverty. The rest of us want to acquire more net worth. We all keep an eye on both roads. The 'enough' fork can come with endings — real or imagined. To avaricious people the 'enough' fork has no end. They will never consider they have enough. Although they are often criticised for everything that goes with being a tall wealth poppy, they really have little control over it because their MA has given them a big dose, so that short of exercising conscious suspension, they will continue to crave acquisition. Less affected people, when looking up the 'enough' fork see an end point where 'enough is enough'.

Recently, my wife bought a lottery ticket which could have won her eighty-million- dollars. When I asked her how she would spend it if she won, she said she would keep a small portion for us to live comfortably for the rest of our lives, but the balance she would give to organisations that she judged were doing good for mankind. So her personal 'enough' had an end point to it. Of course, that may have changed once she was confronted with the money. In any case, further action wasn't required because her ticket turned out to be worthless.

I know a businessman who is well-off — with about twenty-million-dollars of net worth. For most of his early business life he single-mindedly followed the first fork where 'enough' was open ended. But now, in late middle age and living a life that satisfies him, he sees a destination in that fork. It was probably always there, around a corner or in a mist. He may never have looked that far anyway. He still has a way to go to reach it — which he relishes through exercising his business acumen — but quite openly says 'when I do reach it, that will be enough'. Will that be a net worth of thirty-million or fifty-million-dollars? From today's standpoint he could probably put a valid figure on it — although based on the assumption that his needs and outlook will remain unchanged.

People who take the 'enough' fork and reach their defined end, generally stay there. They don't want to return to the dissatisfaction of those stuck in the other fork, burdened with what they see as inadequacy.

A psychiatrist once told me that, based on his clinical experience, nobody gets enough sex. He qualified that by explaining that the 'enough' referred to enough ideal sex. By ideal sex he meant at the time, place, and with a partner of high physical and psychological attraction. He was, in fact, defining the first fork in the sexual road. Up there is a destination comprising the time, place, man, woman or other sexual preference considered to be ideal. And as we know, those preferences will change over time and so will the end point in the sexual 'enough' fork. The rest, being the vast majority, are putting up with what they can get and manage. It may be a partner who represents a reasonable aggregate of qualities they seek but also has deficiencies that won't change. It may be in pornography, where the ideal is always moving out of reach — and too often into illegal territory. Sexual variety is another desire, and one which becomes increasingly expensive as it progresses.

There is a strong argument for the fact that the sexually 'enough' road barely exists, except for those who are born without sexual desire and maintain it throughout their lives. Celibacy, incidentally, is very much in the majority fork of putting up with what they've got — in this case, denial.

'Enough' can be positive or negative when applied to a number of life's experiences. In its positive form we can think of enough net worth — in many manifestations — or enough food, or enough fresh air or enough exercise or enough time. But 'enough' applies equally to negative experiences. On television news there is often a scene outside a courthouse where a judge has just handed down a sentence to somebody found guilty of a crime. Some of those in the street will be shouting that the upcoming incarceration is not enough. When a relationship breaks up a popular expression is 'I'd just had enough.'

Every human positive and negative experience comes, as part of the kit, with the road that forks into 'enough' or 'not enough'. We never stop measuring everything that is happening in our lives by our personal interpretation of whether it is 'enough'. It occupies a great deal of our thinking time and is an elephant in the room of this MA component.

CHAPTER 31

The Pied Piper of Technology

We're changing the world with technology.
Bill Gates

Because change is part of MA, we are propelled by it, whether we like it or not. And as we've discussed, change appears to be speeding up so that one day we may self-destruct or, less pessimistically, turn into something wonderful but unrecognisable to an observer from today. Nobody reading this book will have to witness this event because it is many lifetimes away — which is perhaps a rare benefit of growing old and dying.

Change is now largely tied to technology, which is hurtling forward, out of control. While we may acknowledge this, we are powerless to stop it or even slow it down. On the contrary, we are pouring fuel into its engine.

Like the growth in knowledge, technology was slow to get going early in human history but is now moving at exponential speed. Since this book is an examination of MA, the question arises as to whether technology will change MA, giving humans a new set of behaviours.

Let's take a look at what we define and accept as being human. Science fiction, and especially the ongoing improvement of cinematic special effects, has confronted us with many borderline challenges. My main character in the *Adam Exx* trilogy had his understanding redefined regarding what was acceptable as a woman. Our boundaries are variable. Virtual reality and artificial intelligence are increasingly able to convince us to accept pieces of clever technology as 'human'. Futurists are preparing us for the day when technology is so intertwined with what we used to call 'natural' and 'normal' that the new composites will be as acceptable as unmodified humans are today. In fact, right now, we are passing through the evolutionary portal between human and a human/machine composite. Although we can currently visit the fanciful composite world through virtual reality in its many forms, we can no longer return home to the fundamental and naive humanity of generations past.

CHAPTER 31 The Pied Piper of Technology

Precisely when we left fundamental humanity, is open to debate. It may have been at the time of the Industrial Revolution, or maybe the development of digital data configuration which gave rise to computers. Because civilisations have adopted change at different rates, just as people within those civilisations have, it gets down as much to the individual as it does to the country in which he or she lives. I know many Australians, especially among the elderly, who have not bothered to learn to use a computer or smartphone, thus cutting themselves off from an extension to their personal brainpower and perception. Either they are afraid of, or can't be bothered with, technological change, but are able to survive in relative comfort between now and the end of their lives. While many can master the basics of a simple mobile phone, they run into trouble when they buy new electrical household appliances or cars, because computer driven technology is increasingly confronting and discomforting for the unprepared and untrained user.

Artificial intelligence has already cemented its foundation stone into our humanity. Computers, and especially smartphones, are the most obvious examples. They have dramatically increased our memory capacity, visual recall, communication range and knowledge. I can see a future where each of us we will be able to create and live in our own world. Like winning a lottery, the first reaction to living in a self-created world will be, bring it on! I'll get everything I want, when I want it and how I want it. That will give me endless happiness.

If, as the lore of obstacles postulates, we are given life for the purpose of happiness, then why not use technology to leapfrog over the obstacles and create endless happiness? And the answer is, there can be no ongoing happiness without obstacles to overcome. Yes, we may create our own worlds, but MA will always be fundamental to what we are. This is not to say that the importance and weighting of the components of MA will not change. They have throughout history and will continue to do so in the composite age we're just entering.

It has been suggested by some futurists that here will be a battle between man and machine as computers become self-aware and immensely intelligent. To all intents and purposes, the machine will fit the definition of being alive. But it won't have our MA and therefore it will never be human.

The jury is still out on composites. Let's look at how part human, part machine will deal with MA by briefly going through some of MA's components.

I can't imagine any world or any future where intelligent living organisms will not assemble themselves into a pecking order: in other words, a hierarchy. Technology will have little effect on this. Machines, of course, may develop a system of unified, no-boss behaviour because the individual and the collective are one. But where there is humanity, or indeed any entities that have life as we define it, hierarchies will form. The higher we go in the intelligence chain, the more hierarchies will apply.

As we begin to conquer the challenges of space and the true nature of the universe, we will see size differently. We may be tempted to forget where measurements all began: with the human body. Even though we may regard light years with less awe, or our form may become larger and more powerful than our current human bodies, our historical starting point will remain. Even today, change is noticeable. Our understanding and appreciation of speed and size has broadened immeasurably and will continue to do so even though we still celebrate and admire records that are set using nothing more than the unadulterated, inherited human body.

Will we ever judge our personal worth simply by the attainment of sufficiency? I don't think so, no matter how much technology provides solutions to our needs — real and imagined. We will always look at what those around us have before we assess our own worth. Even in an illusory world, where we could create only positive outcomes for ourselves, we would need to also create a society in which comparisons mattered. Comparisons give rise to competition which gives rise to higher achievement levels.

Crime and punishment are simply two components (or the back and front of one component) that enables the necessary alignment of community behaviour. My hero Sol's MA was virtually dormant when it came to crime and punishment while he lived alone in his cave. If machines eventually take over, there will be no crime because programming will guarantee conformity. If the machines live in communities, they won't need police or prisons — which will make them much more efficient to get on with whatever machines intend to do. But while there are humans or even a significant percentage of humanity in a composite, crime and punishment will endure. Certainly, what is considered a crime and an appropriate punishment will change — as it has over centuries. The current Me-Too movement has created a whole raft of new crimes, some punishable under existing laws and some punishable by public humiliation. The most interesting aspect of Me-Too crime is that it is increasingly based on the personal interpretation of the plaintiff rather than being judged against a set of specific laws as in other parts of the legal system. In one way Me-Too is anti-technology, because it relies so heavily on personality, emotion, and interpretation — with the crowd, led by the media acting as the judiciary.

CHAPTER 31 The Pied Piper of Technology

War is so deeply ingrained into what we are that it is one of the most fundamental components of MA. Wars are being conducted on a small or large scale somewhere in the world all the time. Again, while there is a percentage of humanity left in composites, there will be war. MA dictates that we don't really want peace except to give us time to prepare for the next war. And to complete the irony, what does science fiction do with its miraculous machines? Sends them into battle, of course. We don't often see science fiction presenting peaceful pursuits. And remember that science fiction is one guide to what we would do if we had the power.

Technology is going to bring big changes to life and death as we currently know them, and in doing so will change this component of MA. It has brought about changes already. Not so long ago fifty years marked the beginning of old age. Contrast that with seniors' athletics competitions today for people over ninety. While we're shortening life expectancy with unhealthy lifestyles, we're lengthening it at the other end with medical technology. Currently, you'd have to say that technology is winning. That could go into a dramatic reversal if we keep destroying our environment. Then people would be wiped out and MA would become irrelevant. If that doesn't happen, and technology rockets ahead, we could be like my grandfather's hammer that has had three new heads and two new handles, but is still my grandfather's authentic hammer. With replacement parts and brainpower enhancement we could live for hundreds, if not thousands of years. What I'm suggesting here is a composite of human and machine, but if it retains enough humanity, its MA will change in how it regards and processes life and death.

Can machines love? An interesting question — to which my answer would be no, they can't. And that isn't based on one popular definition of life: 'that which breathes and reproduces itself'. Of course, machines may be programmed to imitate human responses and behaviour. They may copy MA in many other respects, too. My reasoning is based on MA providing susceptibility to catching the love virus. So far in human history love has endured through every peak and trough of living conditions. It is a tough virus and will probably always be part of the human MA mix. Bear in mind that we're talking about romantic love here, not sex. There is no doubt that technology will perfect robots that will make far more efficient sexual partners than humans do now. But that's not romantic love.

Artistry is a component that is probably found only in human MA. While some animals perform dances and sing songs to woo a mate, these could hardly be called works of art. A work of art comes into existence when we interpret the original in another medium. Artistic expression is intertwined with record keeping and advocating; they too are often lumped together. Ancient hieroglyphics, rock paintings and the like may have begun simply as a record, but their antiquity and design elevate them to being regarded as art. The same could be said for commercial art, which combines, art, design and message. Although art is essentially part of human MA, technology will blur the boundaries even further as time passes. While a machine cannot be called an artist, what it produces may be labelled as art, just as a horse's tail dipped in paint and allowed to flick across a blank canvas may be presented as a work of art. We're left with the proposition that art is not only interpreting the original in another medium, but must be accepted by the beholder as art. In effect, this means that artistic expression, to be authentic, must first create a conduit between creator and acknowledger.

The MA directed view of time is unlikely to change so long as it applies to a fully human body — because that's its source. But as we evolve into composites, and lives extend to hundreds, if not thousands of years, the MA relating to time will undergo change. That, of course, may never happen, in which case our original reference to our human bodies and the MA that determines our awareness of time will endure.

Whatever we are, or will become, will always be driven by the MA component of change. In one sense, that part of MA is simply in step with the universe, which itself is continually in a state of change. An interesting question is whether technology brings change or change brings technology. The answer is probably that they are one and the same. Our MA determines that we are irrevocably slaves to change and even if we weren't, our world and the universe in which it exists are going to change anyway. That being the case, the least we can do is acknowledge and accommodate changes such as global warming or cooling. You could say that change is a two-edged sword, one cutting edge is environmental change to which we must react and the other is MA directed change which is specific to our species.

While we remain in our current human form, MA will determine the obstacles and happiness pay-off system that has always dominated human behaviour. Throughout a lifetime, obstacles and pay-offs change, depending upon the progress and events of each individual. No two sets of obstacles and pay-offs are identical, in the same way that no two people are identical. Technology will continue to create more overarching sets of obstacles and payoffs which will run in parallel with our personal sets. After all, they are prompted by MA. But environmental and other externally imposed obstacles will also demand our attention — as they always have.

Blame is another component of MA that seems to be

exclusively human. Animals look purely at events and outcomes. If something nasty happens they appear to deal with it without bothering to accuse who or what might have caused it. That's not to say they don't hand out punishment to those whom they judge as threatening. They learn from adversity and avoid situations that have brought them trouble in the past. But none of this is blame in the human sense. The other side of that coin is that they are attracted to situations that bring them advantage like food, shelter or mating opportunities. Our MA directs us to acknowledge events and outcomes, but then attaches historical cause — which leads to blame. Technology is only interested in cause, effect and reasons. As technology runs increasing portions of our lives, blame will diminish naturally.

Technology will play a vital part in swinging the current dominant position occupied by belief which relies mostly on information from third parties. While the media, assuming the role of gatekeeper, is still driving the dissemination of information, technology is bringing individuals closer to the source of the information. Eighty years ago, we became aware of an air crash by being fed verbal and written accounts of the event by the news media, backed up by black and white photographs. The news was subject to interpretation before it reached us and could have been highly inaccurate. But that was the best we had, and we formed our third-party belief on it.

Nowadays, we have clear, colour video of the crash scene, interviews with aircraft experts, realistic enactments, various degrees and directions of speculation, history and future plans for the airline and the aircraft manufacturer. All this information comes to us from various sources all competing for our attention and purporting to be more accurate than the rest. Short of going to the crash site (if we are vitally interested) our belief in what the media has gathered is probably well placed and will organically become more and more reliable.

The future will see technology more personally driven, taking it to the point where there will be little difference between first-hand belief and third-party belief. As reporting and dissemination of information advances, the current fear of 'fake news' will diminish because the truth will become the only game in town.

Anger arises when our plans and expectations are thwarted. Like fear, technology may relieve us of some current disappointments by solving our problems and taking away the reasons for our anger. But again, like fear, they will be replaced by a new set. There is belief that the more we know the less we fear, that the worst fears come from the unknown. Technology certainly brings increased knowledge which may allay our current fears, but it will supply us with new fears that we cannot yet imagine. So no gain there. Then there are fears that have always been, like the fear of death. Short of providing us with everlasting life, technology will have a tough job removing our fear of death. Even with suicide, assisted or not, a repugnance of continuing life does not cancel out the fear of death — simply because it is an unknown state.

These observations of anger and fear suggest that they are so deeply seated in our MA that technology will do no more than move the goal posts. Other life forms, especially the higher functioning ones, share both fear and anger with us. While they may be more instinctive than intellectual in animals, they remain central to behaviour.

Technology will continue to expand its role in replacing people when it comes to answering questions. Once, we only had people to do the answering. Then we created written records to consult. Libraries became the leading technology in answering. Now we have electronic libraries utilising services like Google to make searching more efficient. Today's shoppers have most of their questions about a product answered by the internet before they walk through the shop doorway — or they may buy online without asking any human a question. None of that suggests technology will remove or even diminish the MA component of questioning. It will certainly shift the role of answering away from other people in real time and become more electronic.

Addictions are like undesirable leaders in politics, countries or religions in that if we could wipe them all out, they would be quickly replaced by another lot — equally as bad. Unfortunately, wholesome replacement leaders are not easily found. The same goes for addictions. While technology will move us toward the elimination of the addictions that are prevalent in today's society, there will be a new crop to replace them because addictions are an irrevocable part of MA. I'm not making a moral judgement on addictions, incidentally. Some of them have been responsible for outstanding strides in human progress, although we might ask ourselves, progress to where? We've slipped back into the discussion about change and, again, we come to the same conclusion, that it is part of MA.

Revenge and forgiveness, although primarily human characteristics, are about making wrong decisions and 'getting even' with people or organisations we judge to have treated us badly. Although technology will have a modifying effect on revenge and forgiveness because it may reduce wrong decisions and make society act more fairly, (both highly subjective terms) other components of MA will work against technology providing a full solution — if indeed we want a full solution. Our MA dictates that we take risks to get ahead, that we embrace luck, that we desire ownership, that we want change. Since these, and many other behavioural patterns cannot always work in our favour, negative outcomes (there will always be plenty of those) will create revenge, whether justified or not. Forgiveness is a more difficult proposition to assign to technology. If technology provides us with more accuracy in measuring cause and effect, then forgiveness will not be needed so much. When we know, with certainty, why something offensive took place, forgiveness is less likely to come up.

Guilt and regret are not likely to be dramatically affected by technology.

Throughout the history of technology our attitude to moral disobedience and wishing something hadn't happened have not changed. While the substance or actions that bring us guilt and revenge have changed, the essence of the MA components have not. Suffering guilt over 'self-rape', as the Catholic Church used to call masturbation, is now much less of a sin than it used to be. The growing trend which is leading to a rise in youth suicide has a whole new set of reasons for guilt, much of it coming from peer pressure. Regret has moved with the times too. We feel regret today in mistreating animals that our forebears found totally acceptable. In my case, I could no longer kill a chicken without serious regret, whereas in my youth I would not have given it a second thought.

One shining attribute of technology is that it cuts down

on the current temptation and dependence on luck. There is so much knowledge — supplied via technology — about every human pursuit, that luck is being put under pressure. The element of luck is being sucked out of business start-ups, babies in the womb, the prices of consumer goods, weather, health — the list goes on. Technology is even encroaching on the luck element in gambling itself, with now so much research and analysis available on likely outcomes. Having said that, I don't believe that humans want to eradicate the notion of luck. I'm tempted to say it is an irrevocable component of MA, but I'm not certain. In all probability we want to indulge in luck, and as technology flushes it out of our current reckoning, we will find new ways to bet in the future.

Ownership has always been part of human MA and that won't change with advancing technology. We all recognise that the billionaire is worth nothing when he lies in a coffin. Ownership is therefore temporary, not that we don't all strive for it in some form or another. While MA will dictate the continuation of ownership, technology will probably change the nature of what we want to own. Once, we might have considered that we owned the money stuffed into our mattress or, before that, the little bags of gold nuggets we hid under the floorboards. Now, ownership is controlled by technology via electronics. Our wealth has been changed to numbers on a screen — although this does not damage our belief in ownership. Even if we own the house we live in, the only factor that prevents us being thrown out by an illegitimate claimant is a written or electronically recorded document we can use as our first line of defence. In the past, without technology, our first line of defence may have been a club or a gun.

Although physical ritual and symbols have remained important elements in the way we live, they too are being moved towards electronics by technology. Our greatest and most personal symbol, our signature, is becoming less and less required as proof of a decision or intent. If we send somebody an email that can be undeniably traced back to us, it is regarded as a legally binding document whether it contains our signature or not.

While ritual is slower to make the transition because it usually requires a physical procedure involving people, symbols are being more quickly modified by technology. For example, the explosive growth in emoji symbols in emails, texts and the internet has replaced great numbers of words.

Imagination is a permanent part of MA and is only enhanced by technology. After all, it was imagination that created all technological advances anyway. In terms of the exercise of imagination, technology provides the tools and the resources for the popular cliché, 'the next level'. Technology, aided by imagination, builds upon itself, sometimes laughing at past simplicities and then challenging the future to produce what imagination has postulated.

As in our consideration of luck, expectation is being increasingly modified by technology. So many of today's expectations are reliant upon technology that we hardly notice it. We expect the train to arrive, or the light to turn on, or the smartphone to provide information and communication. It seldom lets us down, but when it does, we can get angry. That's how strong our expectation is. Technology will continue to make our expectations grow in complexity and become more demanding. The point has already been reached where our expectations far exceed our knowledge of how the bringer of the expectations works. I'm typing these words into a computer which I expect will record it and make it available for modification or transmission. But I only have a vague of idea how this machine works. The same goes for the car I drive. Although I understand the principle of an internal combustion engine, the rest of the technology is beyond me. I simply use it based on expectations. This disconnection between understanding specific technology and simply using it will only widen. Technical specialists will increasingly occupy satellite worlds while they are at work and will return to the general world for their non-professional lives. They will grow more distant from one another, leaving members of the general public only knowing, in principle, what they can do, while the specifics will become an increasing mystery.

Since much of my career has been spent writing about dressing, I have had to observe the changes in fashion over my own decades and also those over past centuries as shown in books and photographic records. Looking at the future, technology will certainly change the fibres we use to make textiles along with the sewing method we have used for centuries to construct clothes. But will the MA dictated practice of dressing to make a statement about ourselves change along with this technology? I doubt it. Aside from more protective apparel becoming necessary for practical reasons, and therefore non-optional, we will go on using clothes to express our personalities and how we see the world.

While technology will change the methods we use for networking, it won't change the MA directed need for it. Once, if we wanted to meet with executives in an international company, we had to fly to a mutually agreed venue. Today we can all be in separate countries and use the facility of an internet conference call. While some people complain that meetings like this miss nuances such as body language, they certainly beat having to sit in an aeroplane for hours just to have a brief meeting in a different country. Technology will advance the way we network by creating 3D facsimiles of ourselves so we can mingle and meet virtually. We're still a long way from 'beam me up' but we have advanced a long way from cricketers having to take a six-week voyage by ship from Australia to play a Test series in England.

As time advances, technology will increase its participation in systems. It's chicken and egg. Without the MA directed necessity for systems, technology would not be organised enough to progress. To be effective, technology must work to a running sheet — which is a definition of a system. An apt metaphor for this relationship can be seen in an automated, mass-production car factory. Imagine all those almost-alive machines lifting, welding and installing car components without a system. The cars that emerged in the end would look like mad sculptures and totally unfit for purpose. The point here is that while technology has evolved as the product of many MA components in combination (most, in fact, play a part), systems is an MA component on its own.

Since uniqueness is an internal view of oneself, technology won't affect it.

Even though technology will increasingly rob us of the satisfaction of rising to physical challenges in favour of pressing buttons, it will free up more time for leisure.

Presumably we will use some of this leisure to pursue personal interests — maybe in artistic expression. The more we achieve in our own development the further it puts us from other people.

The march of technology is turning the concept of 'enough is enough' on its head. Not only has the mix and nature of our assets changed when we tally up our net worth, but so has our understanding of quantity. One of the most profound changes has been in the growing quantity of information available, along with broadening of speculation about the future. A hundred years ago the idea of 'enough' was based largely on life's basic essentials of food, shelter and clothing. The building blocks of those essentials were much simpler, too. My father's first car was an Austin 7. It came with a floor shift gear stick, incandescent lights, canvas-surround windows, a noisy four-cylinder combustion engine fed by a carburettor, rack and pinion direct steering and tyres with inner tubes. Today's cars have replaced all of those components with more advanced ones. More than that, our expectations of future transport are far broader than my father could have imagined. The very idea of 'enough' is now modified similarly. People of my father's era were a lot more certain and satisfied about how much would be regarded as enough. Technology is influencing us to be increasingly less easy to satisfy. There is no point in debating whether this is good or bad. We have no control over it, save the exercise of conscious suspension, which we'll deal with shortly, in which we simply refuse to yearn after more.

CHAPTER 32

MA and the Future

> *The only thing we know about the future is that it will be different.*
> **Peter Drucker**

Just as one of the components of MA is change, MA itself will change — and probably accelerate too, although we have no way of measuring it, except empirically.

The MA we have today is undoubtedly different to that of our distant forebears. Some of that change has been in basics and some brought about by technology. The changes I have observed are less fundamental and more in percentages of the existing. For instance, old-style crime has diminished simply because detection is becoming so much more efficient. Punishment has changed too, moving away from the consequences of physical wrongdoing towards psychological wrongdoing. Who knows how much privacy our ideas will have one hundred years from now and what will be the punishment regime for unlawful intentions or even unlawful thoughts?

MA will continue to change over time, but won't change its pivotal place in our species and that of all living creatures because, without it, we could not function and therefore could not exist.

However, while we can speculate on what will surely be slow changes to MA, it is worth considering where the current package might lead us. Some of MA's components go to make up a deadly cocktail, especially where certain combinations amplify the components. If we list the threats that mankind now faces, we can trace many of them back to MA which, in turn, determines our behaviour — and that has brought us to what many informed people believe is a perilous position. To name a few: food shortages, water shortages, pollution, poisoning of the oceans, climate change (although the degree of human influence is unclear), species extinction, economic chaos, deforestation. Each of these, and many more, have their subdivisions and they make up a frightening picture because we don't seem to be dealing

CHAPTER 32 MA and the Future

with them at a rate that will save us. Fundamental to most of them is overpopulation. More people mean more demands on resources that have a finite size.

Looking at the MA components we've identified, there are some that apply to our survival and others that don't. Let's discuss the major ones that directly influence how long we can live on this planet.

Comparisons lead to excess usage of resources. Desire based on what other people or countries have creates waste because we are deluded in how we measure need. There are two ways of looking at need. One is what is required to maintain life through the provision of food, clothing and shelter. I'm not suggesting that we live like battery hens, but the amount of unused space in our houses, the food that we throw away uneaten and the clothes that we discard simply because we're tired of looking at them are largely brought about by comparisons.

Our continuing engagement in war, for its many reasons and on its many levels, becomes more and more threatening as technology presents us with increasingly pervasive ways of killing each other. Currently, the survival of the human race depends upon a small number of people deciding to withhold using weapons of mass destruction. But, over time, it is likely that a chain reaction of irrationality will unleash

Armageddon. The nasty truth is that war is part of MA, much as we would like it not to be. The same goes for many living creatures whose MA similarly propels them into attacking one another. It is infuriating that the vast majority of people would say they don't want war in principle — but will readily indulge in it if they judge conditions to be intolerable.

Death poses a major threat to life. Before you laugh at this truism, remember that, as we near death, be it from old age or disease, what we can do for the wellbeing of the living who survive us, diminishes. We can't direct their lives after we've gone. The strongest appeals for change come from people who believe they have many years ahead of them. In general, old people lack motivation in trying to change the world's ills — although there are exceptions like David Attenborough who, at ninety-three, was still advocating measures that he argues would save the planet he would soon be leaving.

Change, a fundamental part of MA, has an ambivalent role in the future. Given that change is inevitable, it can be for the good or bad. If we change our attitude to the environment from overuse and waste, to conservation and renewable, then change will work in our favour. The problem here is that change for the good is not going to suit everybody — maybe very few, especially in the short term where most of us live. The energy industry, for example, one of the major contributors to greenhouse gas emissions, is also very rich, influential and a big employer of people whose lives will end naturally, and well before they are seriously affected by climate change. So there is little incentive for them to promote inconvenient change.

The solution, of course, lies in conscious suspension. We have the ability, but seldom the will, to suspend a great number of our MA components. What would it take to convince people to suspend comparisons and war, for instance? I can't see it happening for reasons of morality or even good sense. Religion has failed spectacularly in bringing about a change in behaviour for our general betterment because it has relied on faith for its oxygen rather than practicality. In fact, religion has been a major contributor to conflict and misery.

In all probability, our MA will continue to propel us towards disaster. We will only change course when we begin to lose serious numbers. I'm not suggesting that the human race will be wiped out in one fell swoop, but the survivors will have to learn to practice conscious suspension if they want to go on surviving.

CHAPTER 33

Applying the Knowledge

*Knowledge is of no value
unless you put it into practice.*
Anton Chekhov

This last chapter delivers the payoffs for understanding Mind Architecture. Here you will learn how to use conscious suspension to delete many hazards and enhance your life. You will know how to harness the immense power of your channel and be able to think about thinking. And you will see many of life's obstacles as benefits.

One very important component of our MA is that we have the power to suspend other components — although not all of them. We can't suspend death, for instance, much as we might like to. The success of any conscious suspension is usually dependent upon how long we want the suspension to last. Because MA is the force that determines and drives our behaviour, it naturally imposes itself upon us all of the time. Conscious suspension, therefore, takes continual effort.

Earlier we used the term 'thinking about thinking'. Since all actions are preceded by thought (some of it subconscious) and MA determines the behaviour patterns of those actions, it stands to reason that if we want to suspend undesirable components of MA, we have to tackle them on the thought level. The way to do this is to employ our unique gift of thinking about thinking and deciding to quarantine MA related thoughts that are heading us in the wrong behavioural direction.

Human MA differs from the MA of all other life forms on Earth. We alone have the power of conscious suspension. The behaviour of every other living creature is totally controlled by its MA and its components cannot be suspended.

It doesn't really matter how we achieve conscious suspension, as long as it works. That may be through logical thought, prayer, affirmation or mantra — whatever leads to a resolve we can lock in, for a while at least.

CHAPTER 33 Applying the Knowledge

Some components are easier to suspend than others, while a number are simply not worth suspending at all. Let's look at the possibilities of conscious suspension, using our previous chapters for reference.

Hierarchies are so fundamental to us that we automatically apply them to every situation where there are two or more people. We can consciously suspend hierarchies by seeking solitude, either fully or partly. But we generally find hierarchies are comfortable because they are universally expected and accepted. Unless planned for a specific outcome, conscious suspension has limited use in regard to hierarchies and is seen as little more than being antisocial. The value is in understanding that hierarchies are a major component of MA and will occur wherever there is more than one person. Anticipating a hierarchy gives us a chance to place ourselves in the position we want, whether it be high up in the triangle where we will be a leader or on the base line where few people will bother us. The best time to choose a position is during the formation of the hierarchy before the participants have revealed their power or their intentions.

In some cases, suspension of a hierarchy can be essential for safety. Emperor penguins have a hierarchy, as all animals do, but have learned to suspend it for survival. In freezing weather, a big group will suspend its mating and feeding hierarchy by huddling together and then adopting a slow shuffling system in which each penguin takes a turn on the outside of the group, where it is coldest, in return for a time inside where it is warmest. The penguins know how much tolerance they have for cold and how much need for warmth. If the more powerful pushed their way into the middle of the group while the weaker, on the outside, died of cold, ultimately there would be no protection anyway. In this sense, suspension is helping to maintain the species.

So few people can be detached from calculating size as multiples or divisions of their own bodily dimensions that, for average folk, it is hardly worth suspending. It is only when we need to work in very large or very small numbers that suspension becomes useful. If we are peering through a microscope at a cancer cell or analysing a molecule, we don't relate it to our own body. Neither would our life expectancy have much relevance to the life of a star. In cases like these we need to suspend the link to our own bodies and choose other base lines such as the size of an atom or the speed of light. That happens naturally for people who are engaged in micro or macro-observations. But for everyday use, using our bodies as the starting point works pretty well.

Consciously suspending comparisons has real value

because it cuts out envy — along with some other human failings. Because we assess the worth of people by how successfully they compete, in the broadest sense, we continually compare our life assets with those around us. Whatever we may say, we are dissatisfied with our position. We could always have done better. And the more we dwell on the dual comparisons of what we have achieved, could have achieved and what other people have achieved, the more miserable we will become. The happiness we might get out of contemplating those below us in life assets is outweighed by the unhappiness we get from observing fields that appear greener than ours. This is all going on inside our own heads. We seldom verbalise our happiness in feeling superior or unhappiness in feeling inferior. Nor are we ever taught how to assess and scale life assets. Our method simply forms as we grow up and it varies as much as personalities vary.

Because assessing life assets is private and internal, it follows that conscious suspension must be too. The value of occasionally suspending comparisons benefits us in the way sleep benefits us. We awake refreshed and rebalanced. But while it is relatively easy to go to sleep, suspending comparisons takes conscious effort and resolve.

While suspending comparisons is a matter for personal choice, here are some suggestions that might help. Bear in mind that I do not advocate sitting back, doing as little as possible and expecting the universe will provide.

I have found that verbalising what is good in my life, and what I am thankful for, blocks out comparisons — for a while anyway. The era into which I was born, the country I live in, my friends, my achievements — these are my life assets. I like talking about them and hearing similar assessments from others. In such an exchange, conscious suspension of comparisons occurs naturally. It doesn't last, nor does it have to, because we're only aiming at temporary suspension: a respite from the pressure MA puts us under with comparisons.

Another suggestion. When we are confronted by a comparison — maybe the presence of a high achiever in a field where we have been striving but getting only mediocre results, the temptation is to look at our own failures compared to the life assets of the high achiever. But if we focus on the life assets of the high achiever, admiring and celebrating them, that mindset has the ability to take away the comparison with our life assets. And don't ask me why. It just does.

Because laws, crime, and punishment are consequences of people forming into communities and being buttoned down by MA, personal conscious suspension is not advisable unless we forsake general communal living.

CHAPTER 33 Applying the Knowledge

We can achieve some suspension by choosing to live in a restricted community. For example, crime and punishment are quite different in a convent compared to those in an army.

Of course, what we must remember is that we don't get punished for breaking a law unless we are detected doing so. It has often been said that if everybody who had broken a law had been detected, charged and punished, most of the world's population would be either in jail or paying unbearable fines. It is therefore possible to suspend punishment by not being caught. If you are going to be a crook, at least be a good one. But if you bracket laws, crime and punishment, conscious suspension is a risky choice at best. Rather than suspension, it is better to be familiar with laws so you can comply and avoid punishment.

I'd like to believe that we will eventually suspend war, turning our military expenditure towards solving far more worthy, human and environmental problems. It should happen. But it won't. The reason it won't is that MA will not allow it. Can we stop a rooster from crowing or a dog from barking? No, unless we carry out surgery on them or kill them. The same applies to us. War is here to stay, as it has always been. We all probably favour conscious suspension of war just as we do permanent peace — with some qualifications. But all we can hope for is that our need for war may be turned away from one another and towards external threats to humanity's survival. It can be no more than a hope, because we are ruled by MA. However, acknowledging this will give us the best chance of minimising war and maximising peace.

Can we suspend death or lengthen life? MA will not allow it — so far anyway. At best, technology has lengthened life but at worst has made mass death more possible and threatening than it ever was. As we discussed earlier, the components that make up MA intertwine and this is a prime example. If war prevails, violent deaths increase. If peace prevails, violent deaths decrease. On the flip side, when populations increase, resources are depleted — although that can be offset by technology to a degree. War is only one factor in population volatility.

Technology may one day prolong life more or less indefinitely. But then we have to define 'life'. Is it simply awareness, or does it necessitate a working human body? If the worn-out body I currently possess were replaced with a machine which had my brain and mind in it, would I be less of a person than I am now? If, upon my deathbed, I was offered the opportunity of continuing as 'me' in a machine body, I daresay I would give it a go. At that point I would probably see it as a better alternative than dying — because that is a scary unknown.

But in this day and age, MA serves up life and death. If

CHAPTER 33 Applying the Knowledge

we define 'life' as a collection of experiences, then we can squeeze more into our allocated years. But that's all to do with perception, not the length of time we will live.

Conscious suspension is both relevant and possible when it comes to romantic love. Its success really depends upon how bad a dose of the love virus we've caught. In most cases, love is welcome. Loving our partner or our budgerigar is beneficial to both parties, whereas romantically loving your best friend's spouse can be disastrous. We don't have to worry about suspending romantic love when it will have a good outcome. For those times when the outcome will be bad, conscious suspension is worth pursuing. It can sometimes be achieved simply by an act of will. The boss who has fallen in love with his secretary, and doesn't want to jeopardise his marriage, can arrange to have no further contact with her. That may be by personal agreement or a change of employment for either, but conscious suspension by simply trying to turn it off while still continuing day to day contact probably won't work unless they are prepared to wait for the virus to leave them, and that might result in years of pain.

The best application of conscious suspension of romantic love is to read the warning signs and dive down an escape hatch before the love virus takes hold. Escape hatches are always visible and available, and usually involve the advisory 'don't' word. For instance, don't flirt with somebody inappropriate who is initially attractive to you. Being aware of romantic love virus danger is part of our MA. All we have to do is exercise conscious suspension early enough and the romantic love virus will not gain a foothold. I'm not trying make moral judgements here, incidentally. I'm only showing how to avoid sorrow that can be inflicted by the love virus when it brings negative outcomes. And I'm not talking about lust, either. Although love can be spiced with lust, it doesn't work nearly as well the other way around. Like many addictive substances and activities, lust can become addictive, but it is quite separate from love. Most people continually experience bouts of lust, some more frequently than others.

When we are about to be swept away in swirling floodwaters or engulfed in an oncoming fire, we couldn't care less about artistic expression. The creation, participation and appreciation of the arts needs time that is not taken up with survival. For most people, apart from those full-time professionals creating the art, this means allocating leisure time. And once leisure time is available, the arts compete with myriad other pleasurable pastimes.

But we're considering conscious suspension here and that's easily accomplished by simply not participating. If we refrain from performing music or hearing music in our head, we've suspended it. The same goes for every form of art. We may well ask what is the use of suspending artistic expression? Little, really, unless it consumes us to the point where it threatens our wellbeing.

If we accept time as a physical measure, we cannot suspend it. Staring at a clock and telling it to stop ticking is, literally, a waste of time. But, as we discussed in an earlier chapter, we also work with perceived time — which is quite elastic. The half hour it takes waiting for a bus seems longer than the half hour playing a good game of golf, even though a watch tells us they are exactly the same time interval. And that leads to a conundrum: Happiness shortens perceived time and, as we've said before, perception always beats reality. This brings up another clash with a different component of MA which tells us that we naturally try to elongate our lives and resist death, but doing that with manufactured boredom doesn't make much sense. However, it comes down to a choice. Do we want to be bored for a longer perceived time or engaged and uplifted for a shorter perceived time? We can decide by choosing how to spend our time.

Can we suspend change? Yes, we can, but only so far as it applies to each of us personally. The change that MA forces upon us as a species cannot be suspended. Catastrophes such as wars and global warming may slow it down for a time, but it will eventually resume its acceleration curve. The older we grow, the more we can resist and suspend change as it affects us personally. We can afford to lessen ambition and expectation as we draw closer to death. We can withdraw to familiar places and events and wait out our time with a minimum of change. So, in that sense, we can partly suspend change for ourselves, but not for the world around us.

The longest chapter in this book is about obstacles creating happiness. That doesn't mean it is the most important MA component, although many people will derive more benefit from it than other components we've talked about. In terms of conscious suspension, if we don't formulate our own obstacles our subconscious will do the job for us, and often not to our liking. In this context, conscious suspension becomes conscious creation. If we get lazy and don't consciously create obstacles for pleasurable or satisfying outcomes, our subconscious will step in and our enjoyment of life will take a downturn.

Conscious suspension can be a major benefit once we accept that we all play the blame game, almost automatically. When our plans don't work out or misfortune unfairly strikes us down, MA provides the panacea: blame. The trouble with taking that route is that it bends our personalities down into negative territory so that we begin to expect negative outcomes.

CHAPTER 33 Applying the Knowledge

Every effect has a cause, we know that. It is how we regard the cause that leads us towards or away from blame. The only value in knowing cause is to learn from it. We want to repeat a winning sequence rather than a losing one. That is not easy, but if we suspend blame and simply look at the contributing mechanics of a negative event, we'll be far better off. We can take a lesson from animals. They deal mostly in the world of effect, seldom cause and never blame. MA has let them off lightly.

It is worth remembering that as far as rectifying a negative past event, blame does no good at all. If somebody runs into our car, jumping out and blaming the other driver or the council for placing a power pole in our path, will not take the dent out of the panel. Blame is always a reference to the past and has no bearing on the present or future. Getting into the habit of suspending blame is one of the most valuable takeaways of this book.

While we are virtually powerless to suspend the MA requirement to exercise some belief, there is value in suspending belief in what somebody else tells us rather than that drawn from our own experience. This is not a prompt to reject everything we are told, but rather move it into the temporary file until we have proof it is correct. Most of our beliefs are second-hand. They have arrived via somebody else's utterances. The news media is a prime example. It has been reported to me that the Second World War took place. I was too young to participate in it, so I have no first-hand experience. Do I believe it happened? Based on the number and veracity of reports yes, I believe it did happen. But that is only a belief, not irrefutable, first-hand evidence.

When we look at the body of our third-party beliefs as against first-hand experience beliefs, third-party beliefs account for a dominant percentage. And while this satisfies the demands of MA, it is worthy of some conscious suspension. Men and women go to war and get killed purely on what they have been told. Because we cannot physically experience everything we rely upon, we must believe some of what we are told in order to conduct our daily lives. But there is danger in accepting too much as truth when some of it is untrue and could be dangerous.

While we can suspend both anger and fear, the ability for conscious suspension varies enormously between individuals. In my case, I find it increasingly easy to suspend anger but increasingly difficult to suspend fear — especially on a petty level. I fear running late, or not being able to pay a bill, or not having the physical fitness to play competitive sport. These are fears that in almost every case prove to be unfounded.

MA does provide us with the ability to suspend both

anger and fear, depending upon the circumstances. Anger is the positive and fear the negative, and the most useful conscious suspension is that of anger. It is more likely to have us acting irrationally and place ourselves in danger than fear does.

The great antidote of anger is laughter. We cannot be angry if we're laughing, even inwardly. To laugh when we feel anger pours water on the flames. It won't happen naturally — because we are angry — but we can always find something funny in a situation. We must look for it if we want to suspend anger.

Conscious suspension is simple when it comes to questioning. Just don't talk, but if we have to, don't ask questions. However, that's not a recipe for a happy life. Nevertheless, there are times when no good can come of being involved in a conversation and during those times we can consciously suspend our MA component.

There are many ongoing, public examples of addictions being suspended. On the health and life-threatening level, society pays heavily before and after conscious suspension. This never means permanent and irreversible removal from the addiction, incidentally. Every banished addiction is lying in wait to return to its host, almost as though the addiction has a malevolent life of its own. My wife, even though she has not smoked for thirty years, still labels herself as a smoker who chooses not to smoke.

Although most addictions don't come dressed in the guise of harmful chemicals or unlawful behaviour, they can still ruin our lives by compelling us to repeatedly act outside what is considered normal. It is therefore a useful exercise to frankly monitor our addictions and to apply conscious suspension if they become intolerable to ourselves or those close to us. And we shouldn't be pig-headed enough to resist counselling help if the going gets tough.

While MA subjects us to addictions in general, we can choose to suspend the dangerous ones.

Remorse and revenge are so deeply internalised that they have become what many of us regard as natural and acceptable ways of reacting to events going wrong. Some would regard remorse and revenge as positive behaviour. We often hear the term 'rightful indignation' which might lead us to make remorse and revenge acceptable, expected reactions. The point to remember is that neither remorse nor revenge can affect the event that brought them about. It is in the unchangeable past. Remorse — beating ourselves up about what we should, or shouldn't have done, is self-destructive. And while revenge may bring some

CHAPTER 33 Applying the Knowledge

passing satisfaction in seeing our enemy suffer it is seldom worth the effort.

Every time outcomes go against us remorse, revenge and blame present themselves like troops awaiting battle orders. If we can become conscious of this, we can exercise conscious suspension and send the troops away for a holiday instead of a war.

I've got to admit that trying our luck is often quite good fun. It is only when we follow our MA dictum too deeply into luck so that it takes on a guise of being factual and we hold it responsible for both good and bad outcomes that we should consciously suspend luck. We must console ourselves with what we are witnessing is cause and effect, and usually too complex for us to measure or even contemplate. Blaming good or bad luck is therefore a cop-out. And it does our mental equilibrium good to acknowledge causes that bring us good outcomes. Conversely, rather than blame bad luck we should take the opportunity to discover the causes for bad outcomes so that we might avoid them in future. Luck is very much an MA component that is worth suspending. We do that by reminding ourselves that it is an illusion. Remember the quote from famous film producer Sam Goldwyn: 'the harder I work, the luckier I get.'

Ownership of tangibles seems to become less important

the older we get. Maybe that is because, as we see death approaching, we realise that ownership of objects and wealth will soon be irrelevant to us. That is not the case for intangibles. For some reason we believe that there is a chance we will take those with us — if we believe that we are going somewhere. We hope that the love we have accumulated, our memories and our emotional collection will be in our baggage when we board that last flight. We can suspend ownership of tangibles by giving them away or by directing them to beneficiaries in our Will, but the intangibles cannot be suspended. I don't believe there is a strong case for or against suspending ownership of tangibles.

When we suspend ritual and symbols we are left with the bones of the event, and that isn't always appealing. Here's an example: What is a wedding? It is a lawful agreement uniting two people, and not much different in essence to a business partnership. But ritual and symbols play a major role in most weddings as against very little in business partnerships.

When we boil it down, ritual and symbols become the amplifier of the event and, like any amplifier, they turn small into big. The question arises as to how much ritual and symbols should we tolerate before suspending it. On one hand it is beneficial to know that ritual and symbols are no more than embellishments and we ought to see through

CHAPTER 33 Applying the Knowledge

them to the core. But on the other hand, ritual and symbols exist because MA put them there, so they are an integral part of human behaviour. The compromise is to play both cards; don't confuse the frills for the substance, but enjoy the frills for their entertainment and emotional value.

Imagination is one of the few components of MA that we should never contemplate suspending. But even if we wanted to, it would be virtually impossible. Imagination is so much more than daydreaming or applying creativity to a task. It continually flicks in and out of our consciousness. We use it to prepare ourselves for alternative outcomes. Maybe we have a difficult meeting coming up. What will we say if asked this or that question? What if there is a row and we're asked to leave? Before the meeting we can imagine many scenarios and, in some cases, prepare a response. And, on a loftier plane, imagination has produced virtually every forward (and some backward) move in the evolution of humanity.

If anything, we should encourage imagination in ourselves as well as others. We should also acknowledge its relationship with our channel. Often, when we are trying consciously to imagine a scenario, our channel will take over the task. There is great benefit in developing the link between the two, so that they work as a team: imagination setting up the proposition and the channel coming through with a solution.

Expectation is the brother of imagination, in that before we can expect we must first imagine. Expectation exists in the future and can be controlled, even suspended from action taken in the present. Early in this book we looked at the incredible ability of the human mind to think about thinking. That applies to expectation in that we can suspend it in part. But, like imagination, why would we want to? One reason might be that we are being weighed down by the disappointments of unfilled expectations. When that becomes a burden to the point of depression it is worth looking for some suspension. We might cut ourselves some slack in our golf game, or in our work achievements or in our personal relationships. Expectation is a double-edged sword. While it can be an ingredient of attainment and achievement it can also be a measure of failure.

I suppose my channel dug out dressing as a component of MA because I've been writing about the textile and clothing industry for much of my working life. While my observations about what people were wearing was enough to fulfil what was required of me as a writer on the subject, my deeper curiosity led me to ask why they were wearing certain clothing. We risk being arrested if we suspend the wearing of clothing altogether, so let's forget about that. We can also suspend the daily decision about what to wear by putting on a uniform that relates to our occupation. But that's really skirting around the MA

CHAPTER 33 Applying the Knowledge

dictum rather than confronting and trying to suspend it. The reality is that, because we have to wear something, we have to make a decision about clothing every time we strip down to nakedness. That decision, although often subconscious, makes a statement.

Suspending networking is easy enough. We just have to avoid groups of people. But, like some other possible conscious suspensions, we'd have to ask ourselves: why? Since social interaction can be so productive, switching it off doesn't make sense unless we're trying to hide from accusers or we're too shy to mingle with other people.

We don't have to worry about suspending systems because this happens automatically. Public systems that become outdated are simply abandoned or the zealots for change modify them. Something similar happens to our personal systems. We are continually monitoring them, most of the time unconsciously either creating, tweaking or abandoning them.

Our private feelings of uniqueness can never be suspended. Outwardly, of course, we can appear to be obedient members of whatever organisation we are in, and we can chant its doctrine in unison, but when we are left to our own thoughts, we will always acknowledge our uniqueness. Expressing it may be disadvantageous or even fatal.

One of greatest sources of dissatisfaction is in failing to reach a state of enough in anything we have or do. We could have always had more or done more — and that leads off into infinity. While we may occasionally rest on the belief that we have reached an 'enough' point, for the most part we are nagged by our conscience that we've fallen short, that we will never arrive at that sublime plateau of enough. Conscious suspension offers a way out. In fact, it is one of the most useful exercises when dealing with this challenge that MA thrusts upon us. There are various ways we can go about it. We can, for instance, compare what we need against what we want and, where a need is fulfilled, consign it to 'enough' and put it out-of-mind, remembering that we have the power to think about thinking. We should bear in mind that there is nothing wrong with ambition. It is the anxiety and depression that comes with its non-realisation that does the damage to our happiness.

Employing conscious suspension to nullify some of the MA components that are affecting us adversely is not easy. First, we have to look inward to confront our flaws, construct a list of behaviours we'd like to change, and then identify the MA components that are causing them. Once we've got the enemy into the open, we can take some action.

This might all sound theoretical. You probably agree with it, and want to do it, but where to start? I have a suggestion.

CHAPTER 33 Applying the Knowledge

I'm addressing myself to car drivers, although you could apply the principles of what I am about to say to any situation where multi components of MA act together, often in competition with one another. Driving a car in traffic involves the vast majority of MA components to a greater or lesser or greater extent. This is how they impact.

The driver is in a fluid hierarchy of rights of way, often keenly disputed; size is relevant if you are driving a Fiat Bambino on the same piece of road as a Mack truck; comparisons quickly arise between models, conditions and costs of vehicles, as do driving skills; there are crimes and punishments related to life and property in play; there is war and peace, especially if you listen to the shouts of indignation from opposing drivers and the tooting of horns; time is a governing factor because the calculation of every journey deals with how long it will take; there is anger and fear aplenty; remorse and revenge; there is ownership of space and machines; symbols appear in place of words on signs; there is expectation of traffic flow and everybody obeying the rules; there are systems to turn chaos into order. And let's not forget the star turn of driving: blame! There you have it. Almost every component of MA comes into operation when driving a car in traffic.

Now, here's the suggestion. Next time you get into your car to drive, see how many of those MA components you can suspend. Only toot your horn as a danger warning, not as a rebuke or expression of impatience. Always wave a thank you to the driver who lets you into a line. Don't express anger in any form when another driver does something stupid. It's already in the past; you can't change it by expressing anger. Keep to speed limits and obey road signs and traffic lights. Never, ever get out of your car to fight with anybody over driving; better to apologise even if you are not in the wrong. Admire, rather than envy, cars more beautiful than yours. They are mobile sculptures, some worthy of an art gallery, except you don't have to pay an admission fee. Celebrate the happiness of owning your moving space on the road, of owning life, of sitting in the miraculous machine that is taking you where you want to go.

If you do this exercise only once when driving and then return to your former less-than-admirable self, at least you've experienced conscious suspension. But you may find, as I have, that conscious suspension of certain MA components in driving is worth making permanent. It makes every journey happier, to say nothing of the good feeling spreading to your passengers. And you'll find that some of them will express road-rage on your behalf, even though they are not driving. Take this as a reminder of what you don't want to be like, maybe what you used to be like. That's an MA comparison worth exercising.

CHAPTER 33 Applying the Knowledge

We can also apply this kind of conscious suspension elsewhere. Everybody is driving in the traffic of life. If we look for opportunities for conscious suspension, we'll find plenty. The workplace is full of them. Understanding MA will make us more tolerant of fellow humans. This is not a case of going soft on bad behaviour but at least acknowledging that MA is a hard taskmaster and sometimes impossible to resist. Its components dominate some people more than others. Spare some understanding for those in the grip of nasty compulsions, or those who are acting irrationally because they have been infected by the romantic love virus, or those who are trying to send a message by dressing weirdly. Have some sympathy for those whose expectations are dashed at their feet, or those whose beliefs defy logic and attract ridicule, or those who are overinfluenced by the MA component of ownership which we then read as greed. Yes, all these people can and should exercise conscious suspension, but most don't know about MA and, even if they discovered it, couldn't summon the strength or find the help to nullify a stubborn MA component.

And a final word about channelling. It is worth exploring and exploiting. Even if you can't get your head around MA, you can derive great benefit from getting in touch with your channel and using it. I have mine to thank for writing this book.

www.ingramcontent.com/pod-product-compliance
Lightning Source LLC
Chambersburg PA
CBHW021140080526
44588CB00008B/152